# Panels&Patchwork
## *Quick Quilts for Kids*

LANDAUER BOOKS

# Panels & Patchwork
## Quick Quilts for Kids

Copyright© 2005 by Landauer Corporation
Art Copyright© 2005 by Janet Wecker-Frisch

This book was designed, produced, and published by Landauer Books
A division of Landauer Corporation
3100 NW 101st Street, Urbandale, IA 50322
www.landauercorp.com

President/Publisher: Jeramy Lanigan Landauer
Director of Operations: Kitty Jacobson
Editor in Chief: Becky Johnston
Creative Director: Laurel Albright
Project Designers: Janet Wecker-Frisch and Elizabeth Cecchettini
Contributing Writers: Linda Hungerford and Connie McCall
Technical Writer: Rhonda Matus
Technical Illustrator: Linda Bender
Editorial Assistants: Debby Burgraff, Judy Hunsicker
Photographer: Craig Anderson Photography
We also wish to thank Nancy Nigh, Nancy McClellan and
Sherry Shelden for their project creations and sewing.

Library of Congress Cataloging-in-Publication Data available on request.

This book printed on acid-free paper.
Printed in USA

10-9-8-7-6-5-4-3-2-1

ISBN 10: 1-890621-93-5
ISBN 13: 978-1-890621-93-3

# Introduction

Here and on the following pages treat yourself to quick quilts for kids—22 fast-finish projects with basics, tips & techniques for mixing pre-printed panels and patchwork. Discover how five favorite quilt block patterns from Flying Geese to Pinwheel pair up with pre-printed panels for kids' rooms collections— perfect for personalized birthday or holiday gifts.

Begin by purchasing a simple pre-printed panel design that's ideal for use "as is." (Quilt shops and fabric stores offer a wide variety of panel styles and colors.) Referring to the *Basics* section on pages 8–25, learn how to finish it fast! Start by adding borders to a solo pre-printed fabric panel. Then go beyond basic to combine panels with patchwork, panel motifs with patchwork, and panel fabric coordinates with patchwork. You'll find projects that are easy-sew baby, lap, or twin-sized quilts, pillows, wall or window décor—and even a Christmas crazy quilt and coordinating stocking.

Whether you're already comfortable working with fabric and have "made friends" with your sewing machine, or you're new to sewing and quilting, experience the joy that comes from using pre-printed panels to quickly create bright and artful kid-friendly projects.

# About the Artist

Inspired by her father, talented artist, Janet Wecker-Frisch has been drawing and painting since childhood. She translated her irresistible watercolor illustrations into her own line of ceramic ornaments. Their success led to licenses for wallpaper and border décor, and fabrics. Janet's *Hungry Animal Alphabet*© characters are the inspiration for a best-selling fabric collection created for South Sea Imports®. New collections from Janet Wecker-Frisch, with more on the drawing board, include *Patches & Rhymes*© Mother Goose storybook characters, *Snowfolk Tea Party*©, *Circus Menagerie*© and *Noah's Ark*©.

Janet paints in a studio in her home which she shares with her husband, David. Located in House Springs, Missouri, a suburb of St. Louis, their home is often frequented by visits from their grown children—David, Jacqueline, Katie—and granddaughters—Kaylan and Sydney.

Hungry Animal© Fabric Collection

Circus Menagerie© Fabric Collection

Snowfolk Tea Party© Fabric Collection

Patches & Rhymes© Fabric Collection

# Contents

**I**NTRODUCTION ........3

**A**BOUT THE **A**RTIST ...4

**B**ASICS ...............8

## **P**ANELS WITH **B**ORDERS

Bordered-Panel Quilt .. 28

ABC Panel Quilt ......32

## **P**ANELS WITH **P**ATCHWORK

Flying Geese Quilt .....38

Basic Block Quilt ......42

Pinwheel Quilt .......46

# PANEL MOTIFS WITH PATCHWORK

Pillow & Wall Décor . .52

Big Block Quilt . . . . . . .56

Embroidered Accents . .60

Log Cabin Quilt . . . . . .62

Nine-Patch Pillow . . . .66

Holiday Crazy Patch . . .68
(Quilt & Stocking)

# COORDINATES WITH PATCHWORK

Crazy-Patch Quilt . . . . . . . .76

Box Pillow . . . . . . . . . . . .81

Bolster Pillow . . . . . . . . . .83

Purely Patchwork Pillow . . .86

Multi-Patch Pillow . . . . . . .89

Crib Bumper Pad . . . . . . . .90

Crib Topper . . . . . . . . . . .93

Window Valance . . . . . . . .94

# Basics

◆◆◆◆

$L$earning how to mix pre-printed panels with patchwork will give you more options for many hours of quilting fun—whether you're new to quilting or simply need a refresher. Start by getting acquainted with the many styles of pre-printed panels and their fabric coordinates. Discover how easy it is to make five simple patchwork blocks—Crazy Patch, Log Cabin, Pinwheel, Nine-Patch and Flying Geese—to combine with pre-printed panel motifs and fabric coordinates for a quilt top to baste and tie or quilt.

# What is a Pre-printed Panel?

A pre-printed panel (also known as "cheater cloth") is a large piece of fabric with a stamped design often featuring a familiar theme such as the Mother Goose and Circus panels shown on these two pages. Frequently the center motif sets the scene for the "story" or theme which is carried out to the fabric edge and repeated in coordinating fabrics with prints, stripes, dots, checks, plaids, and all-over "tosses." Accompanying borders ranging from simple to elaborate complete the collection. To make the best use of a panel, be sure to purchase any and all available coordinates for more design possibilities.

# What are Pre-printed Panel Possibilities?

New quiltmakers find panels ideal for practicing basic quiltmaking techniques. Experienced quiltmakers may already have discovered that pairing pre-printed panels with patchwork is perfect for kids' rooms collections, personalized birthday and holiday gifts or a fast-finish charity quilt.

When considering the purchase of a pre-printed panel fabric collection, look closely at the over-all design. A successful pre-printed panel design should incorporate a wide array of characters or stand-alone "motifs" which can be cut out of the panel to mix with patchwork to give the appearance of appliqué.

# What is a Flannel Pre-printed Panel?

Recent improvements in heat-stamping designs onto fabric have made it possible to get excellent detail even on such "fuzzy" fabric as flannel or fleece.

Since flannel's softness is most often associated with infants or toddlers, the pre-printed panel designs are themed accordingly. Traditional pink and baby blue are still in vogue, but bright pastels and even blue and red are quite popular. For baby shower or charity quilt gifts, soft green or yellow are a mainstay. Most often the pre-printed panel in flannel is the size of a standard receiving blanket, like the alphabet panel from the Hungry Animal© flannel collection, above.

# What is a Holiday-themed Pre-printed Panel?

Mixing pre-printed panels with patchwork for festive quilts or wallhangings is a real time-saver during the hectic holiday season. Snowmen themes, such as the Snowfolk Tea Party© shown above, are immensely popular because they can be displayed from late fall throughout the winter months. Look for charming fabric coordinates that can be used for smaller seasonal accessories like table runners and coasters. Here, the predominate blue of the background in the pre-printed panel combines well with Christmas red and green but extends the usefulness of the collection throughout the winter season.

# What Is Patchwork?

Patchwork is any design made of odd pieces of cloth sewn together. Also known as piecing, small bits of fabric are combined to form blocks that subsequently make up a quilt top.

The quilt top, batting, and a backing are layered to form a "sandwich" that is held together by quilting or tying, and then finished with binding along the edges.

Historically, because used clothing was often the only available fabric from which to piece together a bed covering, a creative quiltmaker patched fabrics together to form particular patterns with more visual interest.

Today, an abundant variety of fabrics and techniques offers the quiltmaker endless opportunities for creative sewing expression.

Pre-printed panels are one of many products available today that make it easy to construct a quilt and other decorative accessories.

# What are Five Easy Blocks?

Many of the projects in this book utilize five easily-pieced classic quilt block patterns shown on these two pages. A brief description of each well-known block follows:

Crazy-Patch – In a block made from several irregular pieces, the fabrics are cut randomly, pieced together, and re-cut into the unfinished block size. This is a math-free block with no-fail results.

Log Cabin – This traditional block takes its name from its similarity to the overlapping logs used to construct a cabin. The block is pieced around a center square often cut from red or yellow fabric to represent the warmth of a hearth fire or the light from a window. The remaining rectangles are sewn, one at a time, clockwise or counter-clockwise around the center square.

Flying Geese – Aptly named for the familiar "V" formation of flying geese, this block is rectangle-shaped. It's sewn from one rectangle and two squares of fabric that are pieced with diagonal stitching and then trimmed.

Nine-Patch – Another traditional block, this simple design is just what its name implies— nine fabric patches. Rather than cutting nine individual fabric squares, construct this block following the easy-cut/easy-sew method: Use a rotary cutter to strip-cut three long fabric pieces; sew the strips together; and then sub-cut units to sew into the nine-patch block.

Pinwheel – The similarity to the blades of a windmill or whirl-a-gig, gives the pinwheel block its name. The block is pieced from four half-square triangle patches positioned to appear as though they're spinning.

Crazy-Patch

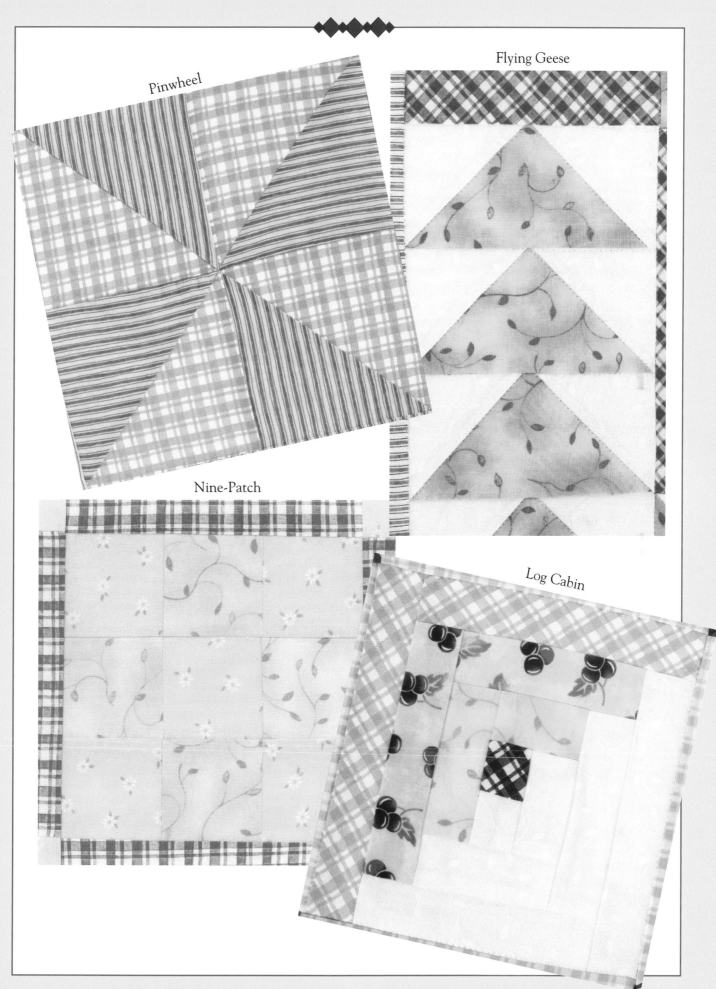

Pinwheel

Flying Geese

Nine-Patch

Log Cabin

15

# Mixing Pre-Printed Panels with Patchwork

To get you started, here are some ideas for creatively combining pre-printed panels and patchwork (pieced) blocks. Use your imagination to develop your own unique designs.

1. Make pieced blocks from small fabric panels. Border each block with complementary fabric strips to create sashing. Or add sashing with small fabric squares at each corner, creating cornerstones.

2. From a small panel cut out one motif from the design. Appliqué this shape to a background fabric or block.

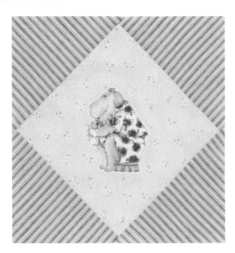

3. Cut out a large motif or several small motifs and appliqué to a complementary background fabric.

4. Choose a motif to place in the center of a block. Called "fussy-cutting," this is how you can select a design to emphasize in your quilt block. Consider adding sashing to make the block larger.

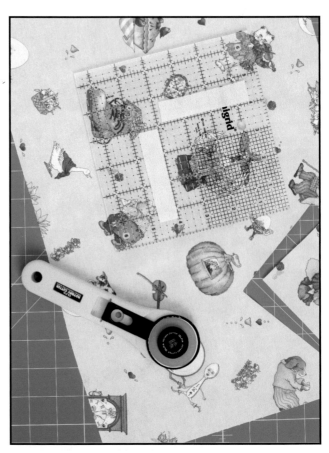

# Rotary Cutting

Rotary cutting is a quick-cutting method for making fabric pieces. Special rotary cutting tools have been designed to make cutting fabric easy and accurate.

For successful quick-cutting, always use a specially designed ruler, mat and rotary cutter. These four items make cutting easy:

1. 6-1/2 x 6-1/2" rotary cutting ruler

2. 6-1/2 x 18" (or 6 x 18") rotary cutting ruler

3. Rotary cutter (45 mm or 60 mm)

4. Cutting mat (at least 24" in length or width)

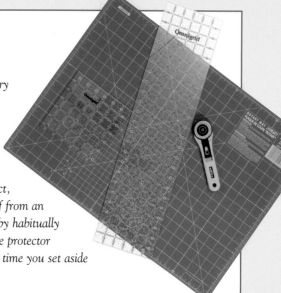

*Caution: Rotary blades are extremely sharp. If your rotary cutter does not automatically retract, protect yourself from an accidental cut by habitually sliding the blade protector into place each time you set aside the cutter.*

# Straightening and Cutting Fabric

Hold the fabric upright to shake out the folds, adjust the edges, and align the selvages. Fold the fabric through the crosswise grain to make the selvages meet, and lay it on your cutting mat. Smooth the fabric, keeping the selvages aligned. Notice that the cut edges—the raw edges—of your fabric may not be aligned.

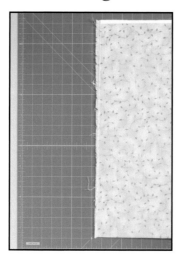

## Straightening Fabric

To straighten the fabric edge, use a 6-1/2" square small ruler as a guide to place a 6-1/2 x 24"-long ruler straight on the crosswise fabric grain.

1. Lay the small ruler along the folded edge, placing one of the marked lines on the fold, and the left side of the small ruler near the fabric raw edge.

2. Place the long ruler beside, and to the left, of the small ruler, butting them together smoothly. The right edge of the long ruler should lay against the left edge of the small ruler.

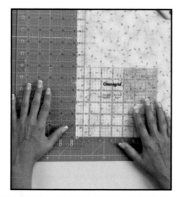

## Cutting Fabric

3. When the rulers are aligned with the fabric fold, pull away the small ruler, keeping your left hand on the long ruler to hold it in position. The long ruler should be positioned so its right edge is inside the raw edge of the fabric. Make sure both layers of the folded fabric will be cut when the small ruler is pulled away.

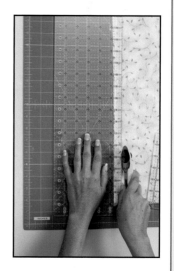

4. Hold the rotary cutter in a vertical position, and with steady pressure roll it along the right edge of the long ruler, from the bottom to the top. As the cutter rolls, walk your fingertips across the surface of the long ruler, maintaining pressure that holds the ruler in place while the rotary blade pushes against it.

When the rotary cutter reaches the top, the raw edge of the cross grain has been cut and straightened.

After the fabric edge has been straightened, you're ready to begin cutting strips and pieces according to the project you've chosen to make.

# Layering and Basting a Quilt

When you have finished your quilt top, here's how to make it into a quilt. A quilt sandwich is made by layering the completed quilt top, quilt batting, and quilt backing. The layers are held together with safety pins, called pin-basting, until the tying or quilting is completed.

## Loft

The loft (thickness) and density of the batting are factors that determine whether you will tie or machine quilt the quilt's layers together. As a general rule, choose less than 1/2" loft polyester batting if you prefer a puffier look that's best for tying together with regularly-placed knots. Choose a low-loft—no more than 1/4" thick—batting if you prefer a flatter appearance. Consider that low-loft cotton batting will move better beneath your sewing machine presser foot than a thicker loft batting. If you're uncertain about which batting to purchase, ask a shop clerk for a recommendation.

## Layering the Quilt Sandwich

To layer the quilt sandwich you'll need:

1. A hard surface work area, preferably at least as large as the quilt backing

*Note: The tips of safety-pins can scratch the work surface, so choose a hard surface that's scratch-resistant. Or, protect the work surface with a rotary mat.*

2. A pressed quilt top with all seams laying flat

3. Batting that measures 4" larger than the quilt top

4. A pressed backing that measures 4" larger than the quilt top

5. Roll of masking tape

6. Safety-pins (1" to 1-1/2" in size)

Be sure the backing fabric has been well-pressed. Then, with the wrong side up, lay it on the surface. Smooth the fabric from the center outward.

To hold the backing securely to the surface place masking tape on one edge, in the middle of the quilt backing. On the opposite side, do the same, being sure not to pull the fabric too tightly.

Complete taping on these two sides. Repeat the process on the remaining two sides, taping every six inches.

Lay the batting on top of the quilt backing, carefully smoothing it from the center outward.

Lay the quilt top on the batting. Be sure that the quilt top and the batting are within the edges of the quilt backing. Check and recheck this before beginning to baste.

## Pin-Basting the Quilt Sandwich

Safety-pins are a quick way to baste a quilt and will hold a quilt sandwich together until the quilt is machine quilted or tied. Safety-pins are best for basting when you expect to accomplish quilting in a short period of time.

Plan to baste with thread when you expect to hand quilt—a quilting process that takes more time to accomplish. For thread-basting, use a sharp needle and thread, and large running stitches made in a spoke wheel or regular grid pattern. An advantage of thread-basting is that thread may be left in a quilt for a longer period of time, whereas safety-pins, when left in a quilt sandwich may leave permanent marks or stains.

## Basting With Safety Pins

Open and scatter safety-pins across the quilt top. With your dominant hand, insert a safety-pin into the quilt top, through all layers of the quilt sandwich. Use both hands to close the safety-pin. Pins can also be closed with a Kwik Clip or other tool such as a grapefruit spoon, held in your not-dominant hand. Insert safety-pins randomly, every four to five inches apart across the quilt top to secure the backing.

# Tying a Quilt

## Tying a Quilt

Tying a quilt is faster than machine quilting, and it's a perfectly acceptable way to finish a quilt. Tied quilts are durable and easily washed, making them great for babies and small children.

## Supplies for Tying

Choose either yarn or heavy thread for tying quilt layers together. Yarn choices include polyester and cotton fibers. Thread choices include embroidery floss and pearl cotton.

You'll also need a sturdy, large-eyed needle. Choose a darning needle, size 14 to 18. The needle eye size will accommodate the thickness of your yarn or heavier thread, and the sharp point will pierce the fabric layers and batting.

## Tying

Cut a length of yarn slightly more than the length of the quilt, using one or more strands to achieve the desired tie thickness. *Note:* If it's expected that a baby will lay on the quilt, consider making small ties that will be more comfortable.

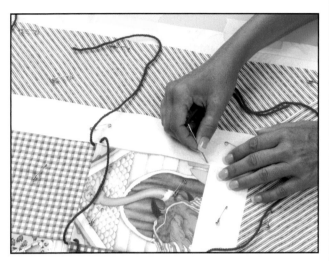

Beginning at the center, as shown above, take an up-down stitch through all three layers of the quilt sandwich—the quilt top, the batting and the backing. Do not cut between stitches. Continue placing a stitch at regular intervals. For easy, no-measuring required ties, place a stitch at the intersection of pieced blocks. This has the added benefit of hiding any mis-aligned blocks.

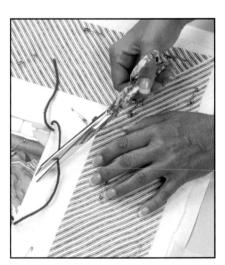

When all the stitches have been made, snip the yarn/thread between each stitch in fairly even lengths.

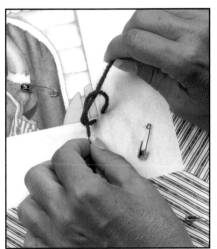

Tie strands right over left, then left over right to make a square knot.

Trim all the ties to a consistent length, approximately 1/2" to 1".

# Quilting by Machine

Machine quilting is a quick and attractive way to quilt. If you've safety-pin basted your quilt sandwich, be sure to remove the pins as you approach the area you want to quilt. Don't attempt to sew over safety pins; you and your sewing machine needle will lose.

Two machine-quilting options are available if you choose to quilt it yourself. You can either sew all straight-line stitches using a walking foot. Or, you can free-motion stitch, sewing curves, circles and other random shapes using only your hands to guide the fabric. For free-motion quilting you'll need a quilting foot.

## Sewing Machine Set-up for Quilting

Set up your sewing machine for quilting. If you plan to straight-line machine quilt, attach a walking foot. If you don't have a walking foot, use your machine's straight stitch foot. For free-motion quilting, attach a darning foot. You'll also need to lower the feed dogs (refer to your sewing machine owner's manual), or cover them so you can move the quilt sandwich smoothly beneath the needle.

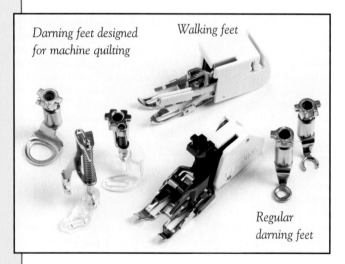

*Darning feet designed for machine quilting*

*Walking feet*

*Regular darning feet*

## Needle for Machine Quilting

Change your sewing machine needle to a quilting needle or a jean's needle, size 80 or 90. This needle has a larger shaft that will more readily puncture the three layers of the quilt sandwich.

## Thread for Machine Quilting

Choose nylon monofilament thread for machine quilting if you want to sew nearly invisible quilting stitches. Thread your sewing machine with the monofilament thread on top and for the bobbin choose a thread color that closely matches the quilt backing. Or, choose the same color of thread for the top and the bobbin. It's helpful to test your stitches before beginning to quilt. Make sure your sewing machine tension is adjusted for your thread (refer to your sewing machine owner's manual).

## Design Options for Machine Quilting— Straight-Line or Free Motion

Simple, straight-line machine quilting, also called utility quilting, is easy to accomplish and will hold the quilt layers together. Whenever possible, begin quilting from the center outward to prevent wrinkles from being quilted into the quilt top or back. Choose from one of these straight stitching options:

1. *Stitch-in-the-ditch quilting.* This quilting requires no marking. Simply stitch along the seam lines as closely as possible.

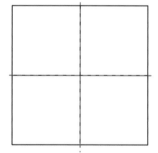

2. *Grid quilting.* Sew a simple grid at regularly spaced intervals on the quilt surface. Align a long rotary ruler with the intersections of blocks. Lightly draw quilting lines with chalk, marking pencil, or a wash-out pen. Quilt on the lines.

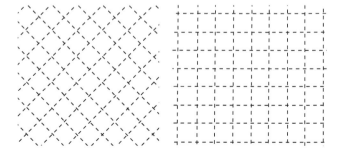

Free-motion quilting is a bit more challenging, but definitely fun. Lower the feed dogs and use a quilting foot for:

3. *Outline quilting.* Stitch around the shape of a motif.

4. *Echo quilting.* After you've stitched to outline a motif, move outward and repeat the quilted outline at regular intervals.

5. *Stipple quilting.* (This is also known as meander quilting.) No marking is needed to create these random curves that flow across a quilt surface.

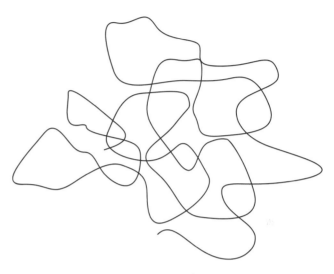

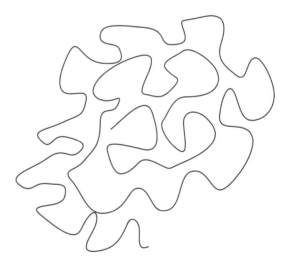

For greater visual interest, try a combination of several quilting designs including straight-line, stitch-in-the-ditch, and free-motion quilting.

# Binding a Quilt

The last step in finishing your quilt is to add the binding. Binding is a fabric strip that encases the outside edges of the quilt. Double-fold binding is most commonly made because it's durable. As the name implies, the quilt edge is wrapped with two layers of fabric. A 2-1/4" to 2-1/2"-wide fabric strip, is folded and sewn to the front of the quilt along the edge, then folded and hand sewn to the quilt back.

If your quilt will hang on the wall, add a sleeve to the top edge of the quilt back at the same time the binding is sewn. (Refer to pages 24 and 25 to simultaneously machine sew the sleeve and binding to the quilt.)

## Overview of Continuous Binding with Mitered Corners

This binding is applied in one long, continuous fabric strip. By folding the binding at each corner, extra fabric is allowed to hand-sew a miter into the corner. See page 41 for detailed instructions.

## Piecing Binding

If you've cut the binding strips according to the pattern instructions, you'll need to sew strips together to obtain the length needed. Here's how:

1. Position a binding strip, right side up, vertically in front of you.

2. To the left and at a perpendicular angle to the vertical strip, position another binding strip right side down on top of the vertical strip.

3. From corner to corner, across the overlapping areas, draw a diagonal line.

4. Sew on the drawn line.

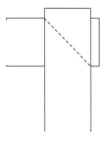

5. Trim away the excess fabric to measure a 1/4" seam allowance.

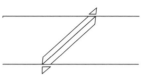

6. Press open the sewn seam to reduce bulk.

7. Fold wrong sides together and press.

## Sewing the Binding to the Quilt Top

Align the raw edges of the binding strip to the raw edge of the quilt top. Sew the binding to the quilt top, using a 1/4" seam allowance.

## Trimming the Quilt Sandwich

After machine sewing the binding to the quilt sandwich, cut away excess fabric and batting. Exercise caution! Be sure to cut away only the excess—not the folded binding or the binding corners.

Place the quilt on the rotary cutter mat with the binding on top. Use the long rotary ruler to measure 3/8" outward from the binding stitching line. Rotary cut along the ruler to remove all but 3/8" of the backing and batting.

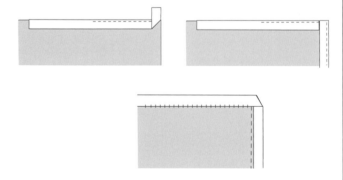

## Hand-Sewing the Binding to the Quilt Back

After trimming away any excess material on the quilt edge, hand-sew the binding in place. Lay the quilt on your lap with the backing facing up. Fold and pin, using metal hair clips, the binding to the back of the quilt.

Knot one end of a needle with thread that matches the color of the quilt backing. Begin hand sewing at any point, securing the binding fold over the machine stitches. Stitch from right to left using a slip stitch.

Take care at each corner to fold and tuck fabric into a diagonal seam, hand-sewing it into place. When the binding and four corners have been sewn down on the quilt back, turn the quilt over and hand-sew the front side of each corner mitered seam.

If you've added a sleeve to your quilt, also hand-sew the folded edge of the sleeve to the quilt back, making sure to take stitches that will not show on the quilt front.

## Finishing: Special Edges

Try one of these special finishes to give the edges of your quilts, pillows, and other accessories a professional, decorative treatment.

1. Piping – A piped edge, especially on a pillow or valance, is a great accent. Simply select cotton cording in a size that is proportional to the size of the finished pillow. You may be able to purchase a pre-sewn cording, called piping, but you can get exactly what you want by sewing bias fabric around cording. Use a complementary print from the panel collection, or choose a contrasting print. Use your sewing machine's zipper foot to sew a straight stitch as close to the cording as possible.

2. Ruffles – Another edging that's especially attractive on pillows and curtains is a ruffle. Whether you choose to add a single ruffle, or stagger two ruffles with the shorter ruffle toward the inside ruffle, a full ruffle looks best. As a general rule, gather one-and-a-half to two times the length of the finished edge to make a decorator ruffle. Lengthen the stitch length of your sewing machine to machine baste; then gather the fabric.

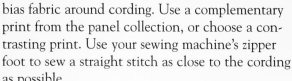

3. Prairie Points – For a special edge on a quilt, curtains, or valance, add prairie points. These can be made individually in a variety of fabric prints and colors to complement your project, or from one print to simply add interest. A prairie point is easily made by cutting fabric squares and folding them—once in half diagonally to create a large triangle, and again in half to make a smaller triangle. Along the length of the quilt, curtains, or valance, equally space, pin, and machine baste triangles to the raw edge. (See page 55 for detailed instructions.)

4. Rick-Rack – Give an interesting edge to a pillow, valance or a quilt by inserting purchased rick-rack into the sewn seam. (See page 83 for detailed instructions.)

# Adding a Hanging Sleeve to a Quilt

To display a quilt on a wall, the best time to add a sleeve or rod pocket to the quilt is at the same time that binding is sewn to the quilt.

The instructions that follow are for creating a sleeve that holds a hidden rod. When the quilt is hung on the wall, nothing is visible except the quilt.

Depending on the size of the quilt you're hanging, you'll need to determine what width of flat lath or molding, or the diameter of the dowel rod you'll need that will reliably support the quilt's weight. A 1" to 2"-wide board gives good support and keeps a quilt flat against the wall. For small quilts, try using a wooden yardstick as a sleeve rod.

## Measure, Cut, and Add a Sleeve

1. Decide which way you want to hang the quilt and measure across the top.

2. Deduct 2" from this number to obtain the finished length of the sleeve.

3. Add 3" to the finished length to obtain the unfinished length. This measurement allows a 1-1/2" fold at each sleeve end.

4. Measure the width of the lath, molding, or dowel used to hang the quilt. Multiply the width by 2, add 1" for ease of insertion, and 1/2" for seam allowances to determine the unfinished width of the sleeve.

5. Using the unfinished measurements, cut out a sleeve from the same fabric as the quilt backing.

6. At each end of the sleeve make a 1-1/2" fold to the wrong side; press.

7. Fold the sleeve length in half, wrong sides together; press.

8. Align the raw edges of the sleeve with the top raw edge of the quilt back. Be sure the sleeve is positioned on the back of the quilt; pin.

9. Align the raw edges of the binding to the top raw edges of the quilt front; pin.

10. Attach the binding and sleeve to the quilt top with a 1/4" seam allowance.

11. Using a slip stitch, hand-sew the folded edge of the sleeve to the quilt back, avoiding taking stitches that will show on the quilt front. Finish by sewing the binding to the back of the quilt.

## Measure, Cut, Drill, and Hang a Board

1. Deduct 1" from the measurement of the quilt top and cut a 1" to 2-1/2"-wide, flat board that length.

2. Approximately 1/3" to 1/2" from each end of the board, drill a hole that will accommodate a nail head.

3. Position the board on the wall and mark the location of the drilled holes.

4. Hammer nails through the marks.

5. Insert the drilled board through the sleeve.

6. Hang the quilt.

## Measure, Cut, and Hang a Dowel Rod

1. Deduct 1" from the measurement of the quilt top and cut a dowel that length.

2. Position the dowel to place marks on the wall 1/4" to 1/3" in from each end of the dowel.

3. Hammer nails through these marks.

4. Insert the dowel rod through the sleeve.

5. Hang the dowel on the nails, making sure the quilt edges cover the nail heads.

Yardstick

Hardwood

Dowel

25

# Panels *with* Borders

**S** tart with a pre-printed fabric panel and you'll be on your way to a finished quilt project in no time at all. Add one, two, or even three borders made from complementary fabrics to increase the size and importance of the quilt. Stitch-in-the-ditch or outline quilt around motifs and printed patchwork designs for a fast faux-patchwork finish.

# Bordered-Panel Quilt

*On a clever pre-printed fabric panel, storybook character motifs and traditional Flying Geese and Pinwheel blocks pair up for instant patchwork. All you add are two borders and quick stitch-in-the-ditch machine quilting.*

## Materials

*Finished size: 41x53"*

1 preprinted character quilt panel
(ours measured
29x43" before trimming)

1/2 yard of yellow plaid fabric
for inner border

2-3/4 yards of border stripe fabric
(with two of the desired border
stripes running length of fabric)
for outer border

1-5/8 yards of yellow print fabric
for backing

3/4 yard of blue stripe fabric
for binding

45x57" piece of quilt batting

Sulky® Polyester Invisible Thread

*All measurements include 1/4" seam
allowances. Sew with right sides
together unless otherwise specified.*

## Cut the Fabric

*For the quilt panel, trim 1/4" beyond the green and white sawtooth border.*

From yellow plaid, cut:
> 2"-wide bias strips to total 145" of inner border

From preprinted border, cut:
> 2—4-1/2x42" outer border strips
> 2—4-1/2x54" outer border strips

From yellow print, cut:
> 1—44x57" backing rectangle

From blue stripe, cut:
> 5—4-1/2x44" binding strips

## Instructions

### Assemble the Wall Quilt Top

1. Sew the short ends of the yellow plaid inner border strips together to form one long strip. Press the seam allowances open.

2. Measure the quilt panel length through the center as shown in Diagram A, and cut two 2"-wide yellow plaid inner border strips to this length. Sew the inner borders to the left and right edges of the panel. Press the seam allowances toward the borders.

*Diagram A*

3. Measure the quilt width through the center including the borders as shown in Diagram B. Cut two yellow plaid inner border strips to this length. Sew the inner borders to the top and bottom edges of the quilt. Press the seam allowances toward the borders.

*Diagram B*

4. To miter the outer border, pin a 4-1/2x54" outer border strip to the right inner border, matching the center of the outer border with the center of the inner border. Sew together, beginning and ending the seam 1/4" from the edges of the inner border as shown in Diagram C. Sew the remaining 54" outer border strip to the left inner border in the same manner. Sew the 4-1/2x42" outer border strips to the top and bottom inner borders. Press the seam allowances toward the outer border strips.

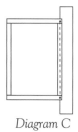

*Diagram C*

5. Working with one corner at a time, draw a diagonal line on the wrong side of the top strip from the corner of the stitching to the point where the two strips meet at the raw edges as shown in Diagram D. Reposition the strips so the bottom strip is on top and draw a second line in the same manner.

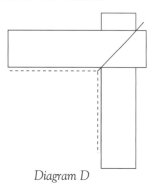

*Diagram D*

6. With right sides together, match the drawn lines and pin as shown in Diagram E. Beginning at the inside corner, sew the outer border strips together directly on the drawn lines. Trim the excess fabric, leaving a 1/4" seam allowance. Press the seam allowances open. Repeat to miter each corner.

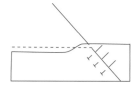

*Diagram E*

## Complete the Wall Quilt

1. Smooth out the backing on a flat surface with the wrong side up. Center the batting on the backing and the quilt top, right side up, on the batting. Baste the layers together.

2. Thread your sewing machine with invisible thread and machine-quilt as desired, beginning in the center and working out to the edges. Our wall quilt was machine-quilted to outline the goose, along most of the preprinted borders and blocks of the panel, and in the ditch along the outer edges of the panel and outer edges of the inner border.

3. Sew the short ends of the 4-1/2"-wide blue stripe binding strips together with diagonal seams to form one long binding strip. Trim the excess fabric, leaving 1/4" seam allowances. Press the seam allowances open. Fold the strip in half lengthwise with wrong sides together; press.

4. Measure to find the quilt width through the center. Use this measurement to cut two binding strips from the blue stripe binding.

5. Aligning the raw edges of the binding with the raw edges of the quilt top, place a binding strip along the top and the bottom edge on the right side of the quilt top. Sew through all layers 1/4" from the raw edges. Trim the batting and backing 1" beyond the binding stitching line. Fold the binding to the back of the quilt to cover the machine stitching; press. Slip-stitch the folded edge of the binding in place or sew in the

ditch along the binding, catching the folded edge of binding on the back of quilt.

6. Measure the quilt length through the center, including the top and bottom binding; add 1" to this measurement. Cut two blue stripe binding strips to this length.

7. Matching the center of the strip with the center of the side edge, sew a binding strip to each remaining edge of the quilt as in Step 5. Trim the batting and backing 1" beyond the binding stitching line. Fold in 1/2" at each end of the binding and fold the binding to the backside of the quilt, covering the machine stitching; press. Slip-stitch or sew in place.

# ABC Panel Quilt

*From Alligator to Zebra, the Hungry Animals on this pre-printed fabric panel are both adorable and zany. To make a wall quilt, border the panel with red check and animal print fabrics. It's as easy as A B Z!*

## Materials

*Finished size: 43x50"*

1 preprinted alphabet block quilt panel
(ours measured 29x42"
before trimming)

3/4 yard of red check fabric for
inner border and binding

2-1/4 yards of blue print fabric
for outer border and backing

46x56" of quilt batting

Sulky® Polyester Invisible Thread

*All measurements include 1/4" seam allowances. Sew with right sides together unless otherwise specified.*

## Cut the Fabric

*For the quilt panel, trim 1/4" beyond the outer alphabet blocks.*

From red check, cut:
  4—2-1/2x44" inner border strips
  5—2-1/4x44" binding strips

From blue print, cut:
  1—44x54" backing rectangle
  4—6x44" outer border strips

## Instructions

### Assemble the Wall Quilt Top

1. Measure the quilt panel width through the center as shown in Diagram A, and cut two 2-1/2"-wide red check inner border strips to this length. Sew the inner borders to the top and bottom edges of the panel. Press the seam allowances toward the borders.

*Diagram A*

2. Measure the quilt length through the center, including the top and bottom borders as shown in Diagram B. Cut two red check inner

border strips to this length. Sew the inner borders to the left and right edges of the quilt. Press the seam allowances toward the borders.

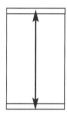

*Diagram B*

3. Using the length found in Step 2, cut two outer borders from the 6"-wide blue print strips. Referring to Diagram C, sew the outer borders to the left and right edges of the quilt. Press the seam allowances toward the outer borders.

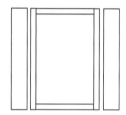

*Diagram C*

4. Measure the quilt width, including all borders. Cut two outer borders to this length from the remaining blue print strips. Sew the borders to the top and bottom edges of the quilt as shown in Diagram D. Press the seam allowances toward the outer borders.

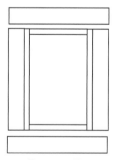

*Diagram D*

## Complete the Wall Quilt

1. Smooth out the backing on a flat surface with the wrong side up. Center the batting on the backing and the quilt top, right side up, on the batting. Baste the layers together.

2. Thread your sewing machine with invisible thread in both the needle and the bobbin. Refer to Diagram E to machine-quilt between the vertical and horizontal rows of alphabet blocks and in the ditch along the outer edges of the panel and outer edges of the inner border. Quilt a 2-1/4" diagonal grid in the outer border.

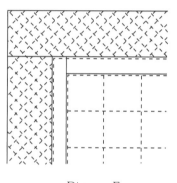

*Diagram E*

3. Sew the short ends of the binding strips together with diagonal seams to form one long binding strip. Trim the excess fabric, leaving 1/4" seam allowances. Press the seam allowances open. Fold the strip in half lengthwise with wrong sides together; press.

4. Beginning at the center bottom of the quilt, place the binding strip on the right side of the quilt top, aligning the raw edges of the binding with the raw edges of the quilt top. Fold over the beginning of the binding strip about 1/2". Sew through all layers 1/4" from the raw edges, mitering the corners. Trim away the excess binding, leaving 1/2" at the end to overlap the beginning of the strip. Trim the batting and backing even with the quilt top.

5. Fold the binding to the back of the quilt to cover the machine stitching; press. Slip-stitch the folded edge of the binding in place or sew in the ditch along the binding, catching the folded edge of binding on the back of quilt.

# Receiving Blanket

To add a soft finishing touch, trim a flannel pre-printed
panel with white satin prairie points for a
memorable receiving blanket to welcome baby.

# Panels *with* Patchwork

*P*airing pre-printed fabric panels with patchwork is a quilter's dream—traditional quilt block patterns such as Flying Geese, Log Cabin and Pinwheel add ingenuity and interest to a panel-centered quilt.

# Flying Geese Quilt

*When choosing a pre-printed fabric panel, let your imagination soar.*
*Choose a classic block pattern that enhances the panel's theme—such as*
*surrounding a charming Mother Goose motif with Flying Geese blocks.*

## Materials

*Finished size: 50-1/2x55-1/2"*

10-1/2x15-1/2" rectangle from preprinted character panel

3-1/2 yards of blue print fabric for section rectangles and backing

1-5/8 yards of white-on-white fabric for Flying Geese squares

1-1/2 yards of blue-on-blue fabric for Flying Geese rectangles

1 yard of blue plaid fabric for bias strips

1/2 yard of blue stripe fabric for binding

55x60" piece of quilt batting

Sulky® Polyester Invisible Thread

*All measurements include 1/4" seam allowances. Sew with right sides together unless otherwise specified.*

## Cut the Fabric

From the blue print fabric, cut:
  2—30-1/2x55" backing rectangles
  2—5-1/2x25-1/2" horizontal section rectangles
  2—5-1/2x30-1/2" vertical section rectangles

From white-on-white, cut:
  18—3x44" strips; from the strips cut
  232—3" flying geese squares

From blue-on-blue, cut:
  17—3x44" strips; from the strips cut
  116—3x5-1/2" flying geese rectangles

From the blue plaid fabric, cut:
  3"-wide bias strips to total 225"; from the strips cut
  2 each of the following lengths:
  33", 25-1/2", 20-1/2", 10-1/2", 8", and 5-1/2"
  4—5-1/2" bias-cut squares

From blue stripe, cut:
  6—2-1/2x44" binding strips

# Instructions

## Assemble the Flying Geese Rows

1. With right sides facing, place a 3" white-on-white square on the corner of a 3x5-1/2" blue-on-blue rectangle. Draw a diagonal line on the square as shown in Diagram A. Sew on the drawn line and trim the seam allowance to 1/4". Press the seam allowance toward the white-on-white triangle.

*Diagram A*

2. Sew another white-on-white square to the opposite corner of the blue-on-blue rectangle in the same manner, creating a Flying Geese unit as shown in Diagram B. Repeat to make a total of 116 Flying Geese units. The pieced rectangles should measure 3x5-1/2".

*Diagram B*

3. Sew together the Flying Geese units to make two rows of 11 for the horizontal sections, two rows of 13 for the vertical sections, two rows of 16 for the top and bottom borders, and two rows of 18 for the left and right borders. Refer to Diagram C to assemble the Flying Geese rows with all units in the same direction, pressing the seam allowances toward the long edge of the blue triangles.

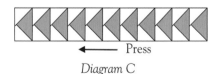

*Diagram C*

## Assemble the Quilt Center

1. Sew a 10-1/2" blue plaid bias strip to the top and bottom edges of the Mother Goose rectangle. Press the seam allowances away from the center. To complete the Mother Goose section, sew a 20-1/2" blue plaid bias strip to the remaining two edges of the rectangle as shown in Diagram D. Press the seam allowances away from the center.

*Diagram D*

2. Refer to Diagram E for the two horizontal sections and assemble each in the numerical order shown. Sew a 25-1/2" blue plaid bias strip (1) to one long edge of each 5-1/2x25-1/2" blue print horizontal section rectangle (2). Next sew an 8" blue plaid bias strip (3) to one end, creating an L with the blue plaid strips. To complete each horizontal section, sew an 11-unit Flying Geese row (4) to the remaining long edge of the blue print rectangle so the blue triangles point away from the bottom of the L.

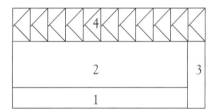

*Diagram E*

3. Refer to Diagram F for the two vertical sections and assemble each in the numerical order shown. Sew a 5-1/2" blue plaid strip (1) to a 5-1/2 x30-1/2" blue print vertical section rectangle (2). Next sew a 33" blue plaid bias strip (3) to one long edge, creating an L with the blue plaid strips. To complete each vertical section, sew a 13-unit Flying Geese row (4) to the remaining long edge of the blue print rectangle so the blue triangles point away from the bottom of L.

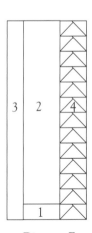

*Diagram F*

4. With right sides facing, sew a horizontal section to the Mother Goose section, aligning the remaining long edge of the Flying Goose row with the bottom edge of the Mother Goose section. Begin sewing 2" from the right edge of the Mother Goose section and stop at the left edge as shown in Diagram G. Press the seam allowances away from the center.

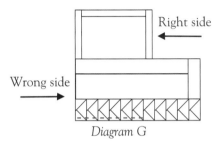

*Diagram G*

5. Working in a clockwise direction, add a vertical, horizontal, and vertical section to the center unit in numerical order as shown in Diagram H. Press all seam allowances away from the center. To finish, complete the bottom seam, sewing from the previous stitching to the right edge of the last vertical section.

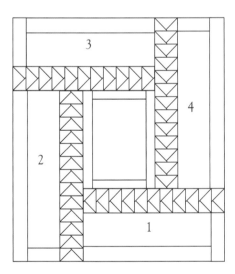

*Diagram H*

## Assemble the Quilt Top

1. Sew an 18-unit Flying Geese row to the left and right edges of the quilt center so the triangles point up on the left edge and down on the right edge. Press the seam allowances away from the borders.

2. Sew a 5-1/2" blue plaid square to each end of the two 16-unit Flying Geese rows as shown in Diagram I.

Press the seam allowances toward the squares. Sew the pieced borders to the top and bottom edges of the quilt center so the triangles point right on the top and left on the bottom. Press the seam allowances away from the borders.

*Diagram I*

## Complete the Quilt

1. Sew together the long edges of the 30-1/2x55" blue print backing rectangles with a 1/2" seam allowance. Press the seam allowances to one side.

2. Smooth out the backing on a flat surface with the wrong side up and center the batting on the backing. Center the quilt top, right side up, on top of the batting. Baste the layers together.

3. Thread your machine with invisible thread and machine-quilt through all layers beginning in the center and working outward, sewing in the ditch along the edges of all the pieces. In addition, machine-quilt to outline the goose.

4. Sew the short ends of the 2-1/2"-wide blue stripe binding strips together with diagonal seams to form one long binding strip. Trim the seam allowances to 1/4" and press open. Fold the strip in half lengthwise with wrong sides together; press.

5. Beginning at the center of the bottom edge, place the binding strip on the right side of the quilt, aligning the raw edges of the binding with the raw edges of the quilt top. Fold the beginning of the binding strip about 1/2". Sew through all layers 1/4" from the raw edges, mitering the corners. Trim away the excess binding, leaving 1/2" at the end to overlap the beginning of the strip. Trim the batting and backing even with the quilt top.

6. Fold the binding to the back of the quilt to cover the machine stitching; press. Slip-stitch the folded edge of the binding in place or sew in the ditch along the binding, catching the folded edge of the binding on the back of the quilt.

# Basic Block Quilt

*To build this easy block quilt, start from the center with a flannel pre-printed panel patchwork of animal blocks. Scatter same-size alphabet blocks along the border and machine-appliqué in place.*

## Materials

*Finished size: 61x70-1/2"*

2 panels of preprinted animal patch flannel fabric for quilt center

1-5/8 yards of yellow small floral print flannel fabric for outer border

1-1/4 yards of green check flannel fabric for corner squares, inner border, and binding

1/2 yard each of green, blue, and cream large alphabet flannel fabric for appliqués

3-1/2 yards of green alphabet flannel fabric for backing

Twin-size quilt batting

Sulky® Rayon or Poly Deco Decorative Thread in blue, green, red, and yellow

Paper-backed fusible webbing

Sulky® Tear-Easy stabilizer

Sulky® KK 2000 temporary spray adhesive

Sulky® Polyester Invisible Thread

*All measurements include 1/4" seam allowances. Sew with right sides together unless otherwise specified.*

## Cut the Fabric

*For the preprinted animal patch, trim 1/4" beyond the outer animal patches for the quilt center.*

From yellow small floral print, cut:
    4—8-1/2x58" outer border strips

From green check, cut:
    4—8-1/2" corner squares
    5—2-1/2x44" inner border strips
    7—2-1/2x44" binding strips

From the large alphabet flannels, cut:
    22 appliqué squares or rectangles, centering an animal/letter in each shape and combining J/K, U/V, and X/Y (we cut 7 cream, 7 blue, and 8 green)

## Instructions

### Assemble the Quilt Top

1.  Measure to find the width of the animal patch quilt center as shown in Diagram A, and cut two 2-1/2"-wide green check inner border strips to this length. Sew the inner borders to the top and bottom edges of the quilt center. Press the seam allowances toward the borders.

*Diagram A*

2. Measure the quilt length through the center including the borders as shown in Diagram B. Seam the 2-1/2"-wide green check inner border strips as needed to make two this length. Sew the inner borders to the left and right edges of the quilt center. Press the seam allowances toward the borders.

*Diagram B*

3. Using the length found in Step 2, cut two 8-1/2"-wide yellow small floral outer border strips. Sew the outer borders to the left and right edges of the quilt as shown in Diagram C. Press the seam allowances toward the outer borders.

*Diagram C*

4. Measure the quilt width, including all borders, and cut two 8-1/2"-wide yellow small floral outer border strips to this length. Sew an 8-1/2" green check corner square to each end of each outer border as shown in Diagram D. Press the seam allowances toward the borders. Sew the pieced borders to the top and bottom edges of the quilt. Press the seam allowances toward the outer borders.

*Diagram D*

## Complete the Quilt Top

1. Smooth out the batting on a flat surface. Center the quilt top, right side up, on top of the batting. Pin the layers together.

2. Thread your sewing machine with green decorative thread. Machine-quilt the yellow small floral print

outer borders in a 1-1/2" diagonal grid as shown in Diagram E.

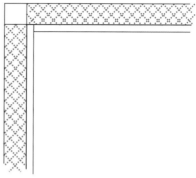

*Diagram E*

3. For each alphabet appliqué square and rectangle, cut a corresponding shape of fusible webbing. Fuse webbing to the wrong side of each shape, following the manufacturer's instructions. Remove the paper backing.

4. Spread the quilt top right side up on a flat surface. Use the photograph on page 42 as a guide to position the appliqué shapes on the outer borders. Place A-E on the top border, F-L on the right side border, M-Q on the bottom border, and R-Z on the left side border. When you are happy with the positioning, pin the shapes in place.

5. Cut pieces of tear-away stabilizer slightly larger than the fused shapes. Center stabilizer behind the fused shapes on the back of the quilt top with temporary spray adhesive. Satin-stitch over the edges of the shapes with yellow decorative thread. For an added touch, use a second color of decorative thread to machine-buttonhole stitch directly over the satin stitching. Tear away the stabilizer.

## Complete the Quilt

1. For the backing, cut the 3-1/2-yard length of green alphabet flannel fabric in half crosswise, making two 1-3/4-yard lengths. Sew together the selvage edges, using a 1/2" seam allowance. Trim off the selvages and press the seam allowances to one side.

2. Smooth out the backing on a flat surface with the wrong side up and center the quilt top, batting side down, on the backing. Baste the layers together.

3. Thread your machine with green decorative thread. Beginning in the center and working outward, machine-quilt between all of the preprinted animal patches on the quilt center. Rethread the machine with invisible thread and quilt in the ditch along both edges of the inner border and the corner squares as shown in Diagram F.

*Diagram F*

4. Sew the short ends of the 2-1/2"-wide green check binding strips together with diagonal seams to form one long binding strip. Trim the seam allowances to 1/4" and press open. Fold the strip in half lengthwise with wrong sides together; press.

5. Beginning at the center of the bottom edge, place the binding strip on the right side of the quilt, aligning the raw edges of the binding with the raw edges of the quilt top. Fold the beginning of the binding strip about 1/2". Sew through all layers 1/4" from the raw edges, mitering the corners. Trim away the excess binding, leaving 1/2" at the end to overlap the beginning of the strip. Trim the batting and backing even with the quilt top.

6. Fold the binding to the back of the pillow to cover the machine stitching; press. Slip-stitch the folded edge of the binding in place or sew in the ditch along the binding, catching the folded edge of the binding on the back of the quilt.

# Pinwheel Quilt

*Pieced pinwheels border a pre-printed fabric panel that takes center stage with a performing menagerie for this circus-themed bed quilt. The pre-printed, crazy-pieced corner blocks add to the whimsy.*

## Materials

*Finished size: 66-1/2x83-1/2"*

17-1/2x35-1/2" rectangle from preprinted Circus Menagerie© quilt panel

5-1/4 yards of blue medium-print fabric for backing and B strips

1-1/2 yards of monkey stripe border fabric for C strips

1-1/4 yards of green dot fabric for H strips and blocks

1 yard of pink large-print fabric for F strips

1 yard of red dot fabric for binding and blocks

5/8 yard of yellow dot fabric for E strips

5/8 yard of yellow diamond fabric for D strips and corner rectangles

1/2 yard of green medium-print fabric for G strips

1/2 yard of pink dot fabric for blocks

1/2 yard of pink medium-print fabric for blocks

3/8 yard of pastel stripe fabric for blocks

1/4 yard of blue dot fabric for A strips

74x90" piece of quilt batting

Sulky® Polyester Invisible Thread

*All measurements include 1/4" seam allowances. Sew with right sides together unless otherwise specified.*

## Cut the Fabric

From blue medium-print, cut:
- 1—44x90" backing rectangle
- 2—17x90" backing rectangles
- 2—3-1/2x17-1/2" B strips

From monkey stripe border fabric, cut:
- 5—6x52-1/2" C strips

From green dot, cut:
- 5—5-1/2x44" H strips
- 2—3-5/8x44" strips; from the strips cut 16—3-5/8" block squares

From pink large-print, cut:
- 4—7-1/2x44" F strips

From red dot: cut:
- 8—2-1/2x44" binding strips
- 2—3-5/8" strips; from the strips cut 16—3-5/8" block squares

From yellow dot, cut:
- 4—5x44" E strips

From yellow diamond, cut:
- 2—5x33-1/2" D strips
- 4—3x3-1/2" corner rectangles

From green medium-print, cut:
- 3—4-1/2x44" G strips

From pink dot, cut:
- 3—4-3/8x44" strips, from the strips cut 24—4-3/8" block squares

From pink medium-print, cut:
- 3—4-3/8x44" strips, from the strips cut 24—4-3/8" block squares

From pastel stripe, cut:
- 2—4-3/8x44" strips, from the strips cut 16—4-3/8" block squares

From blue dot, cut:
- 2—3x35-1/2" A strips

# Instructions

## Assemble the Pinwheel Blocks

1. With right sides together, layer the 3-5/8" squares in pairs, using a red dot with each of the green dot squares. Cut the layered squares in half diagonally as shown in Diagram A to make 32 sets of triangles.

*Diagram A*

2. Sew 1/4" from the diagonal edge of each pair as shown in Diagram B to make a square. Press the seam allowances toward the red triangles.

*Diagram B*

3. Arrange sets of four squares as shown in Diagram C. Sew the squares together in rows and then sew the rows together to make 8 red/green dot pinwheel blocks.

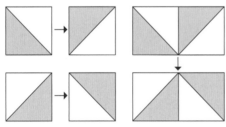

*Diagram C*

4. Repeat Steps 1–3 with the 4-3/8" squares to make 12 pink print/dot pinwheel blocks and 4 pastel stripe pinwheel blocks. For the pastel stripe blocks, layer the squares with the stripes running in the same direction.

## Assemble the Quilt Top

1. Use the Quilt Assembly Diagram, opposite, as a guide to assemble the quilt top. Sew a blue dot A strip to the left and right edges of the Circus Menagerie rectangle. Press the seam allowances away from the center.

2. Sew a 3x3-1/2" yellow diamond corner rectangle to each end of each blue medium-print B strip as shown in Diagram D. Press the seam allowances toward the B strips. Sew the pieced B strip/corner rectangles to the top and bottom edges of the quilt. Press the seam allowances away from the center.

*Diagram D*

3. Sew together the red and green pinwheel blocks to make two rows of 4 blocks as shown in Diagram E. Press all seam allowances the same direction. Sew the block rows to the top and bottom edges of the quilt. Press the seam allowances away from the block rows.

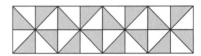

*Diagram E*

4. Sew a monkey stripe border C strip to the left and right edges of the quilt; press the seam allowances away from the center.

5. Sew the yellow diamond D strips to the top and bottom edges of the quilt.

6. Seam the 5"-wide yellow dot strips as needed to make two 61-1/2" E strips. Sew the E strips to the left and right edges of the quilt. Press the seam allowances away from the center.

7. Seam the 7-1/2"-wide pink large-print strips as needed to make two 61-1/2" F strips. Sew the F strips to the left and right edges of the quilt. Press the seam allowances away from the center.

8. Sew together the pink pinwheel blocks to make two rows of 6 blocks. Sew a pastel stripe pinwheel block to each end of each row. Press all the seam allowances the same direction. Sew the block rows to the top and bottom edges of the quilt. Press the seam allowances away from the block rows.

9. Seam the 4-1/2"-wide green medium-print strips as needed to make two 56-1/2" G strips. Sew the G

strips to the top and bottom edges of the quilt. Press the seam allowances away from the center.

10. Seam the 5-1/2"-wide green dot strips as needed to make two 83-1/2" H strips. Sew the H strips to the left and right edges of the quilt. Press the seam allowances away from the center.

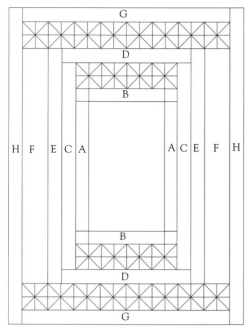

*Quilt Assembly Diagram*

## Complete the Quilt

1. Trim off the selvage from the backing rectangles. Sew a 17x90" backing rectangle to each long edge of the 44x90" backing rectangle with a 1/2" seam allowance. Press the seam allowances away from the center of the backing.

2. Smooth out the backing on a flat surface with the wrong side up and center the batting on the backing. Center the quilt top, right side up, on top of the batting. Baste the layers together.

3. Thread your machine with invisible thread and machine-quilt through all layers beginning in the center and working outward. Quilt along the design lines of the Circus Menagerie rectangle and in the ditch along the outer edges of the rectangle. Quilt in the ditch along all edges of the pinwheel blocks and along the edges of each strip. Quilt two lines to divide the A, E, G, and H strips into thirds and quilt diagonal lines 1-1/4" apart across the F strips.

4. Sew the short ends of the 2-1/2"-wide red small-print binding strips together with diagonal seams to form one long binding strip. Trim the seam allowances to 1/4" and press open. Fold the strip in half lengthwise with wrong sides together; press.

5. Beginning at the center of the bottom edge, place the binding strip on the right side of the quilt, aligning the raw edges of the binding with the raw edges of the quilt top. Fold the beginning of the binding strip about 1/2". Sew through all layers 1/4" from the raw edges, mitering the corners. Trim away the excess binding, leaving 1/2" at the end to overlap the beginning of the strip. Trim the batting and backing even with the quilt top.

6. Fold the binding to the back of the quilt to cover the machine stitching; press. Slip-stitch the folded edge of the binding in place or sew in the ditch along the binding, catching the folded edge of the binding on the back of the quilt.

# Panel Motifs
## with Patchwork

W

Whether a pre-printed fabric panel features one design motif or a dozen different motifs, each design becomes the inspiration for an entirely new quilt when combined with patchwork blocks. You can also pair up panel motifs with decorative edgings such as ruffles and prairie points and embellish with machine embroidery accents.

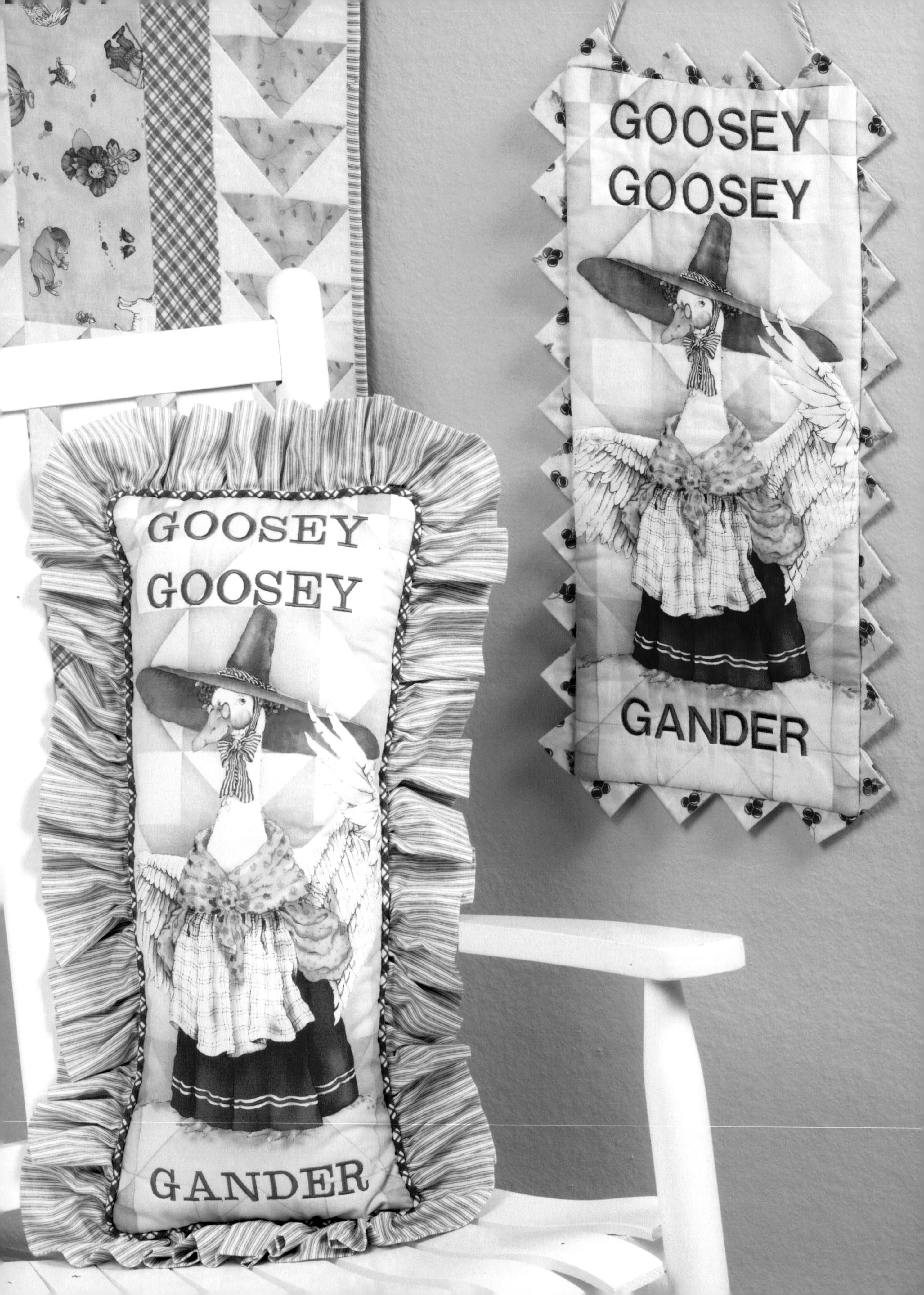

GOOSEY
GOOSEY
GANDER
GOOSEY
GOOSEY
GANDER

# Pillow & Wall Décor

*Goosey goosey gander, wither do you wander? Onto a quick ruffled pillow and easy wall décor—each accented with edging and machine-embroidery. Simply replace the goosey goosey gander embroidery with the child's name or nickname to personalize.*

## Materials

*Finished size: 41x53"*

1 1/4 yards of blue stripe fabric for back and ruffle

10-1/2x23" center motif rectangle from preprinted character panel for pillow front

1-3/4"-wide bias strips of red plaid fabric to total 2 yards of piping

Sulky® Tear-Easy stabilizer

Sulky® KK 2000 temporary spray adhesive

Sulky® Rayon or Poly Deco Decorative Thread in blue

11x24" piece of lightweight batting

Sulky® Polyester Invisible Thread

2 yards of 1/4"-diameter cotton cording

Polyester fiberfill

*Sew with right sides together, using 1/2" seam allowance unless otherwise specified.*

# Ruffled Pillow

## Cut the Fabric

From blue stripe, cut:

    1—10-1/2x23" back rectangle,
    with the stripes running the long direction
    3—7x44" ruffle strips

## Instructions

1. Referring to the photograph, opposite, machine-embroider "Goosey Goosey" above the goose and "Gander" below the goose on the pillow front with 1"-tall letters using stabilizer and blue decorative thread. For information about embroidering, refer to pages 60 and 61.

2. Center the pillow front right side up on batting and baste 1/2" from pillow front edges. Thread your sewing machine with invisible thread and quilt as desired. Our pillow front was machine-quilted to outline the goose and then the shawl.

3. Sew the short ends of the piping strips together to form one long strip. Press the seam allowances open. Center cording on wrong side of strip and fold fabric over cording, matching long edges. Use a zipper foot to sew through both fabric layers close to the cording.

4. Beginning at the bottom edge of the pillow front, pin piping to the right side of the front, slightly rounding corners with raw edges facing out and seam line of piping atop basting stitches.

Clip seam allowance of piping at corners for a better fit. Overlap ends of piping, trimming off excess piping. Sew piping to pillow front using zipper foot.

5. For ruffle, sew the 7" edges of the ruffle strips together to form a big circle. Press the seam allowances open. With wrong sides together, fold the strip in half lengthwise and press. Sew gathering threads through both layers 1/2" and 1/4" from the raw edges. Pull on the gathering threads until the circle of ruffle fits around the perimeter of the pillow front as shown in Diagram A, slightly rounding the corners. Adjust the gathers evenly, pushing a little extra into the corners of the pillow. Pin and sew the ruffle to the pillow front.

*Diagram A*

6. Sew the pillow front to the back atop the ruffle sewing line, leaving a 6" opening in the bottom edge.

7. Trim the seam allowances and turn the pillow cover right side out. Stuff the pillow cover firmly with polyester fiberfill. Sew the opening closed.

# Materials

*Finished size: 41x53"*

10-1/2x23" center motif rectangle from preprinted character panel for front

10-1/2x23" rectangle of coordinating fabric for back

1/3 yard of yellow print fabric for points

1-1/4x19" bias strip of blue stripe fabric for hanger

Sulky® Tear-Easy stabilizer

Sulky® KK 2000 temporary spray adhesive

Sulky® Rayon or Poly Deco Decorative Thread in blue

11x24" piece of lightweight batting

Sulky® Polyester Invisible thread

*All measurements include 1/2" seam allowances. Sew with right sides together unless otherwise specified.*

# Wall Decor

## Cut the Fabric

From yellow print fabric, cut:
28—3-1/2" squares

## Instructions

1. Referring to the photograph, opposite, machine-embroider "Goosey Goosey" above the goose and "Gander" below the goose on the wall hanging front

with 1"-tall letters using stabilizer and blue decorative thread. For information about embroidering, refer to pages 60 and 61.

2. Center the wall hanging front right side up on batting and baste 1/2" from wall hanging front edges. Thread your sewing machine with invisible thread and quilt as desired. Our wall hanging front was machine-quilted to outline the goose and then the shawl.

3. For the prairie points, refer to Diagram A. Fold each 3-1/2" square in half diagonally with wrong sides facing and press. Fold it in half again, forming a smaller triangle and press.

*Diagram A*

4. Pin the prairie points to the wall hanging front, aligning the long raw edge of each prairie point with the raw edge of the wall hanging front as shown in Diagram B. Begin at the center of a side edge, overlapping the points slightly by slipping the folded edge of a prairie point into the open side of the adjacent triangle. Adjust the overlap as needed to fit ten points on each side edge and four on the top and bottom edges. Sew the points to the front.

*Diagram B*

5. To make the hanger, fold the blue stripe bias strip in half lengthwise with right sides together. Sew with a 1/4" seam allowance, leaving the short edges open. Trim the seam allowance to 1/8", turn right side out, and press.

6. Pin the hanger ends to the right side of the wall hanging front, aligning the raw edges with the raw edge of the wall hanging front. Place an end 1" in from each top corner as shown in Diagram C. Sew the ends in place along the prairie point seam.

*Diagram C*

7. Sew the wall hanging front to the back atop the point basting line, leaving an opening in the bottom edge.

8. Trim the seam allowances and turn the wall hanging right side out. Sew the opening closed.

# Big Block Quilt

*This extra-long twin quilt features a patchwork of checked blocks embellished with randomly-placed embroidered letters, plus your choice of eight alphabet blocks from a pre-printed fabric panel.*

## Materials

*Finished size: 65x99"*

Preprinted alphabet
block quilt panel for appliqués

1/3 yard each of check fabric
in blue, green, pink, red,
and yellow for center squares

1/3 yard each of small floral
print fabric in blue, green, pink,
and yellow for center squares

1/3 yard each of stripe fabric in blue,
green, and yellow for center squares

2-1/4 yards of cream floral print
for inner border

2-7/8 yards of blue print
for outer border

6 yards of yellow large-print
for backing and binding

73x106" piece of quilt batting

Sulky® Tear-Easy™ stabilizer

Sulky® KK 2000
temporary spray adhesive

Sulky® Rayon or Poly Deco™
Decorative Thread in
blue, green, red, white, and yellow

Sulky® Puffy Foam™
in blue, green, red, and yellow

Sulky® Polyester Invisible Thread

*All measurements include 1/4"
seam allowances. Sew with right sides
together unless otherwise specified.
The border strips are cut longer than
needed and trimmed later to allow for
individual differences in piecing.*

## Cut the Fabric

From quilt panel, cut:
    8—7" alphabet blocks

From the 1/3 yard fabrics, cut:
    9—12" letter squares (we cut 3 blue, 3 green,
        1 red, and 2 yellow)
    36—9" center squares (we cut 8 blue, 8 green,
        8 pink, 3 red, and 9 yellow)

From cream floral, cut:
    2—2-1/2x80" inner border strips
    2—2-1/2x45" inner border strips

From blue print, cut:
    2—9-3/4x102" outer border strips
    2—9-3/4x48" outer border strips

From yellow large-print, cut:
    1—44x103" backing rectangle
    2—14x103" backing rectangles
    3"-wide binding strips to total 9-1/2 yards

# Instructions

## Assemble the Quilt Center

1. Cut sixteen 12" squares of tear-away stabilizer. Use temporary spray adhesive to center two layers of stabilizer on the back of each 12" letter square. Machine-embroider a 4-3/4"-tall letter centered on each of the stabilized squares using decorative thread and matching Puffy Foam. Refer to the photo and Quilt Assembly Diagram for ideas on combining thread and fabric colors. Tear away the stabilizer. Trim each embroidered square into a 9" square, centering the letter. For more information about embroidering, refer to pages 60 and 61.

2. Lay out the center blocks on a flat surface, including the embroidered letter squares, in 9 rows of 5 blocks, using one letter square in each row. Arrange the blocks as desired or use the Quilt Assembly Diagram as a guide.

3. When you are pleased with the arrangement, sew the blocks together in rows. Press the seam allowances of each row to one side, alternating the direction with each row.

4. Sew the rows together to complete the quilt center.

5. For each alphabet block square, cut a 7" square of fusible webbing. Fuse webbing to the wrong side of each alphabet block, following the manufacturer's instructions. Trim each block into a 6-1/2" square and remove the paper backing.

6. Spread the quilt center right side up on a flat surface. Referring to the Quilt Assembly Diagram, position the appliqué blocks on the quilt, centering each over an intersection of four center squares. When you are happy with the arrangement, pin the blocks in place. Fuse the blocks to the quilt.

7. Cut squares of tear-away stabilizer slightly larger than the fused blocks. Center a piece of stabilizer behind each fused shape on the back of the quilt center with temporary spray adhesive. Satin-stitch over the edges of each block with white decorative thread. For an added touch, use a second color of decorative thread to machine-buttonhole stitch directly over the white satin stitching. Tear away the stabilizer.

## Assemble the Quilt Top

1. Measure to find the quilt width through the center as shown in Diagram A. Cut two 2-1/2"-wide cream floral inner border strips to this length. Sew the inner borders to the top and bottom edges of the quilt center. Press the seam allowances toward the borders.

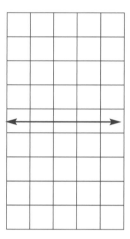

*Diagram A*

2. Measure the quilt length through the center including the borders as shown in Diagram B. Cut two cream floral inner border strips to this length. Sew the inner borders to the left and right edges of the quilt. Press the seam allowances toward the borders.

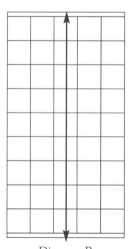

*Diagram B*

3. Measure to find the quilt width through the center, including the inner border. Use this measurement to cut two outer borders from the 9-3/4"-wide blue print strips. Referring to the Quilt Assembly Diagram, sew the outer borders to the top and bottom edges of the quilt. Press the seam allowances toward the outer borders.

4. Measure the quilt length through the center, including all borders. Trim the two remaining blue print outer borders to this length. Sew the borders to the left and right edges of the quilt. Press the seam allowances toward the outer borders.

## Complete the Quilt

1. Sew a 14 x103" backing rectangle to each long edge of the 44 x103" backing rectangle with a 1/2" seam allowance. Press the seam allowances away from the center of the backing.

2. Smooth out the backing on a flat surface with the wrong side up and center the batting on the backing. Center the quilt top, right side up, on top of the batting. Baste the layers together.

3. Thread your machine with invisible thread in both the needle and the bobbin. Machine-quilt through all layers beginning in the center and working out to the edges. Refer to Diagram C to quilt between the vertical and horizontal rows of center squares. Quilt around each appliqué block and in the ditch along the outer edges of the quilt center and the outer edges of the inner border. Quilt a 3" diagonal grid in the outer border.

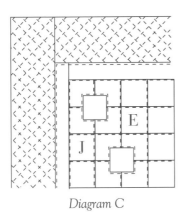

*Diagram C*

4. Sew the short ends of the 3"-wide binding strips together with diagonal seams to form one long binding strip. Trim the excess fabric, leaving 1/4" seam allowances. Press the seam allowances open. Fold the strip in half lengthwise with wrong sides together; press.

5. Beginning at the center of one edge of the quilt, place the binding strip on the right side of the quilt top, aligning the raw edges of the binding with the raw edges of the quilt top. Fold over the beginning of the binding strip about 1/2". Sew through all layers 1/2" from the raw edges, mitering the corners. Trim away the excess binding, leaving 1/2" at the end to overlap the beginning of the strip. Trim the batting and backing even with the quilt top.

6. Fold the binding to the back of the quilt to cover the machine stitching; press. Slip-stitch the folded edge of the binding in place or sew in the ditch along the binding, catching the folded edge of binding on the back of the quilt.

*Quilt Assembly Diagram*

# Embroidered Accents

*Embroidered accents will personalize almost anything. Our basic instructions offer tips for easy machine-embroidered letters and border accents for quilts, pillows and accessories.*

◆◆◆◆◆

## Materials

Fabric to be embroidered

Sulky® Tear-Easy™ stabilizer

Sulky® KK 2000
temporary spray adhesive

Chalk or air-erasable marker

Sulky® 40 wt. Rayon or
Poly Deco™ Decorative Thread

2mm-thick Sulky® Puffy Foam™
to match decorative thread

## Instructions

1. Cut your fabric at least 1" larger than the desired finished size. This will enable you to trim the fabric to the desired size after the embroidery is complete, ensuring that the letter can be centered on the fabric.

2. To stabilize the fabric, cut two pieces of tear-away stabilizer the same size as the fabric. Spray a light coat of temporary spray adhesive between the two layers of stabilizer. Spray the top layer of stabilizer and place the fabric, wrong side down, on the top layer. Smooth all layers together.

3. Mark the center of the fabric with chalk or air-erasable marker. Hoop the fabric, following the machine manufacturer's instructions. The fabric should be taut. Take care not to pull or distort the fabric when hooping.

4. Select an embroidery letter style with wide satin columns. Outline font styles are a good choice because they are fully enclosed with no open ends on the columns. Another option is tapering open ends.

5. Place hooped fabric on the machine, aligning the foot with the center mark. Cut a piece of Puffy Foam slightly larger than the area to be embroidered. Place the Puffy Foam under the foot and lightly hold it in place until the first few stitches tack it in place. Or, apply a light coat of temporary spray adhesive to the back of the Puffy Foam before placing it on the hooped fabric. Stitch through all layers.

6. When the embroidery is complete, remove the hoop from the machine. Carefully tear away the excess Puffy Foam along the perforations made by the stitching. If the embroidered design has areas without perforations from stitching, use a scissors to trim the Puffy Foam close to the embroidery. To shrink little fuzzies of Puffy Foam along the edges of the embroidery, hold a steam iron about 1/2" above them and shoot them with steam.

The embroidered letters on several of the featured projects were sewn with a computerized embroidery machine. Extra dimension was added to give the letters a padded look using Sulky® Puffy Foam™. The Puffy Foam™ perforates cleanly when stitched through, and makes the stitching stand well above the fabric. Before embroidering the block, test sew over an extra piece of Puffy Foam™ on a scrap of stabilized fabric.

# Log Cabin Quilt

*Motifs cut from a pre-printed fabric panel like the charming storybook characters featured here blend well with traditional Log Cabin blocks arranged in a classic Ohio Star pattern.*

◆◆◆◆◆

## Materials

*Finished size: 43x43"*

Fabric with large motifs to fill
4—7-1/2" squares and
1—6x8" rectangle

1-3/4 yards of yellow plaid fabric
for prairie points,
background rectangle, and log strips

3/4 yard of green plaid fabric
for sashing

5/8 yard of white-on-white fabric
for log strips and block squares

1/2 yard of red plaid fabric
for center squares and sashing squares

1/8 yard of yellow small-print fabric
for log strips

1/8 yard of yellow-on-yellow fabric
for log strips

1-1/4 yard of yellow medium-print
fabric for backing

42x42" piece of quilt batting

Paper-backed fusible webbing

10x12" rectangle of Sulky Tear-Easy
stabilizer

Sulky KK 2000 temporary
spray adhesive

Sulky Rayon or Poly Deco Decorative
Thread in yellow

Sulky Polyester Invisible Thread

*All measurements include 1/4" seam
allowances. Sew with right sides
together unless otherwise specified.*

## Cut the Fabric

From large motif fabric, cut:
> 1—6x8" center rectangle, centering a motif in the rectangle
> 4—7-1/2" block squares, centering a motif in each square

From yellow plaid, cut:
> 32—6" prairie point squares
> 1—8x10" bias-cut background rectangle
> 1-1/2"-wide bias strips to equal a minimum of 120" for logs

From green plaid, cut:
> 8—2-1/2x40" strips; from the strips cut
> 40—2-1/2x7-1/2" sashing strips

From white-on-white, cut:
> 6—1-1/2x40" log strips
> 4—7-1/2" block squares

From red plaid, cut:
> 25—2-1/2" bias-cut sashing squares
> 8—1-1/2" bias-cut center squares

From yellow small-print, cut:
> 2—1-1/2x40" log strips

From yellow-on-yellow, cut:
> 2—1-1/2x40" log strips

From yellow medium-print, cut:
> 1—42" backing square

From fusible webbing, cut:
> 1—8x10" rectangle
> 1—6x8" rectangle

63

# Instructions

## Assemble the Log Cabin Blocks

1. Sew the 1-1/2" red plaid center squares to a 1-1/2"-wide white-on-white log strip as shown in Diagram A.

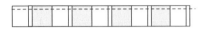

*Diagram A*

2. Cut the strip even with the edges of the center squares as indicated in Diagram B. Press the seam allowances away from the center squares.

*Diagram B*

3. Place the two-square units on another white log strip as shown in Diagram C, so the center squares follow the white squares as you sew. Cut the strip even with the two-square units, forming three-piece units. Press the seam allowances away from the center squares.

*Diagram C*

4. Continue adding logs in this manner, positioning the units on the strips so the last log attached is the first as you sew. Add logs in the following order: 2 yellow-on-yellow, 2 white-on-white, 2 yellow small-print, 2 white-on-white, and 2 yellow plaid. Make 8 log cabin blocks as shown in Diagram D.

*Diagram D*

## Assemble the Quilt Top

1. Lay out the log cabin blocks, block squares, sashing strips, and sashing squares on a flat surface, using the photograph on page 62 as a guide.

2. To make the block rows, sew together the blocks and sashing strips as indicated in Diagram E. Press all seam allowances one direction.

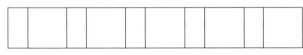

*Diagram E*

3. To make the sashing strips, sew together the sashing strips and sashing squares as indicated in Diagram F. Press all seam allowances the opposite direction from the block rows.

*Diagram F*

4. Sew the block rows and sashing strips together; press.

5. Fuse a corresponding webbing rectangle to the wrong side of the yellow plaid background rectangle and the motif rectangle, following the manufacturer's instructions. Remove the paper backing. Center and fuse the yellow plaid rectangle on the quilt top and the motif rectangle on the yellow plaid rectangle.

6. Center the stabilizer rectangle behind the fused yellow background rectangle on the back of the quilt top with temporary spray adhesive. Satin-stitch over the edges of each rectangle with yellow decorative thread.

## Complete the Quilt

1. For the prairie points, refer to Diagram G. Fold each 6" yellow plaid square in half diagonally with wrong sides facing and press. Fold it in half again, forming a smaller triangle and press.

*Diagram G*

2. Pin the prairie points to the right side of the quilt top, aligning the long raw edge of each prairie point with the raw edge of the quilt top as shown in Diagram H. Begin at the corner of an edge, overlapping the points slightly by slipping the folded edge of a prairie point into the open side of the adjacent triangle. Adjust the overlap as needed to fit 8 points on each edge. Sew the points to the quilt top.

*Diagram H*

3. Smooth out the backing on a flat surface with the wrong side up and center the batting on the backing. Center the quilt top, right side up, on top of the batting. Baste the layers together.

4. Thread your machine with invisible thread and machine-quilt through all layers beginning in the center and working outward. Refer to Diagram I to quilt in the ditch along each sashing seam; do not quilt in the sashing along the edges of the quilt top.

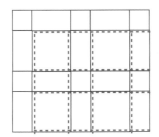

*Diagram I*

5. Trim the backing and batting even with the raw edge of the quilt top. Trim an additional 1/4" of batting from each edge. Turn the prairie points out to point

away from quilt top, folding the raw edges of the quilt top over onto the batting. Fold under 1/4" on the edges of the backing. Slip-stitch the folded edge of the backing in place or sew in the ditch along the prairie points, catching the folded edge of backing on the back of the quilt.

# Nine-Patch Pillow

*The classic Nine-Patch gets updated when you add a character motif from a pre-printed panel and rag the seams to create a fun fringe. This is one of the few times where sewing the wrong sides of the fabric together works!*

## Materials

1/2 yard of yellow print fabric

1/4 yard of red plaid fabric

Fabric with motif to fill a 6" square for front center

14x14" pillow form

*Sew with WRONG sides together together using 1/2" seam allowances unless otherwise specified.*

## Cut the Fabric

From yellow print, cut:
    1—16" back square
    4—6" front squares

From red plaid, cut:
    4—6" bias-cut front squares

From motif fabric, cut:
    1—6" center front square,
    centering the motif in the square

## Instructions

1. Lay out the 6" squares on a flat surface in 3 rows of 3 squares, placing the motif square in the center and alternating the print and plaid squares around the center square.

2. Sew the squares together in rows, and then sew the rows together to complete the pillow front.

3. To fringe, make 1/4" to 3/8" cuts 1/4" apart along the sewn seams of the pillow front.

4. Sew the pillow front to the back, leaving an 8" opening in the bottom edge.

5. Insert the pillow form into the pillow cover. Use a zipper foot to sew the opening closed, sewing 1/2" from the raw edges. Fringe the outer seam allowances of the pillow cover as in Step 3.

# HolidayCrazy Patch

*Waiting for Santa's visit couldn't be more comfy with a quilt for snuggling and a stocking for stuffing. Here, motifs cut from the pre-printed fabric panel Snowfolks Tea Party© is in full swing on an easy-to-patch crazy quilt.*

## Materials

*Finished size: 59x59"*

2/3 yard of preprinted Snowfolk's Tea Party© fabric for appliqués

3-1/4 yards of Snowfolk's border stripe fabric (with two of the desired border stripes running length of fabric) for outer border

2-1/4 yards of red check for prairie points and blocks

3/4 yard of yellow check for inner border and blocks

1 fat quarter each of blue, red, and yellow dot fabrics for blocks

1 fat quarter each of blue and green large-print fabric for blocks

1 fat quarter of gold-stars on-blue fabric for blocks

1 fat quarter of green small-print fabric for blocks

3-3/4 yards of green check for backing and blocks

2-1/2 yards of muslin for foundation squares

58x58" piece of quilt batting

Sulky® Polyester Invisible Thread

*All measurements include 1/4" seam allowances. Sew with right sides together unless otherwise specified.*

## Holiday Quilt

### Cut the Fabric

From the preprinted Snowfolk's Tea Party© cut:
    1 to 3 square or rectangle appliqués for each of the 9 blocks

From border stripe, cut:
    4—5-1/2x56" outer border strips

From red check, cut:
    10—6x44" strips; from the strips cut
    56—6" prairie point squares
    9 irregular-shaped pieces with straight edges for blocks

From yellow check, cut:
    2—1-1/2x42-1/2" inner border strips
    3—1-1/2x44" inner border strips
    9 irregular-shaped pieces with straight edges for blocks

From each fat quarter fabric, cut:
    9 irregular-shaped pieces with straight edges for blocks

From green check, cut
    2—29-1/2x58" backing rectangles
    9 irregular-shaped pieces with straight edges for blocks

From muslin, cut:
    9—16" foundation squares

### Instructions

*Assemble the Crazy Blocks*

1. Select 7 or 8 irregular-shaped pieces in a variety of colors and patterns for one block. Place one

*Diagram A*

shape, right side up, on a muslin foundation square as shown in Diagram A; pin in place.

*Diagram B*

2. With right sides facing, align a second shape along one edge of the first shape; pin in place. Sew the shapes together through all three layers as shown in Diagram B. Flip the second shape so it is right side up; press.

*Diagram C*

3. Position the third shape so one of its edges is in a straight line over the first two shapes as shown in Diagram C; sew 1/4" from this edge. Flip the third shape so it is right side up; press.

4. Continue adding shapes in this manner, completely covering the muslin foundation. Shapes that extend beyond the edges of the foundation square will be trimmed later. In some cases it may be necessary to fold under some edges of a shape and hand-appliqué those edges in place. Also, hand-appliqué on shapes to fill odd-shaped areas, covering any exposed muslin.

5. Trim the crazy block to measure 14-1/2" as shown in

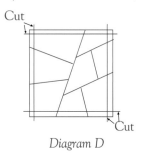

*Diagram D*

Diagram D. Baste 1/4" from the raw edges.

6. Repeat Steps 1-5 to make 9 crazy blocks.

## Assemble the Quilt Center

1. Lay out the crazy blocks in three rows of three bocks on a flat surface, turning the blocks to vary the position of the colors throughout the quilt until you are pleased with the arrangement.

2. Press under 1/4" along all edges of each preprinted appliqué square or rectangle. Position 1 to 3 appliqués on each block, using Diagram E as a guide. Thread your sewing machine with invisible thread. Working

with one block at a time and replacing it when finished to hold its position, edge-stitch the appliqués on the blocks.

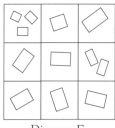

*Diagram E*

3. Sew the blocks together in rows. Press the seam allowances of each row to one side, alternating the direction with each row.

4. Sew the rows together to complete the quilt center. Press the seam allowances toward the center row.

## Assemble the Quilt Top

1. Sew the 1-1/2x42-1/2" yellow check inner border strips to the top and bottom edges of the quilt center. Press the seam allowances toward the borders.

2. Sew the short ends of the remaining yellow check inner border strips together to form one long strip. Press the seam allowances open; cut two 44-1/2"-long inner border strips.

3. Sew the 44-1/2"-long inner borders to the left and right edges of the quilt. Press the seam allowances toward the borders.

4. To miter the outer border, pin a 5-1/2x56" outer border strip to an inner border, matching the center of the outer border with the center of the inner border. Sew together, beginning and ending the seam 1/4" from the edges of the inner border as shown in Diagram F. Repeat with each outer border. Press the seam allowances toward the inner border.

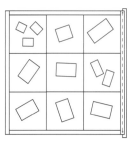

*Diagram F*

5. Working with one corner at a time, draw a diagonal line on the wrong side of the top strip from the corner of the stitching to the point where the two strips meet at the raw edges as shown in Diagram G. Reposition the strips so the bottom border is on top and draw a second line in the same manner.

*Diagram G*

6. With right sides together, match the drawn lines and pin as shown in Diagram H. Beginning at the inside corner, sew the outer border strips together directly on the drawn lines. Trim the excess fabric, leaving a 1/4" seam allowance. Press the seam allowances one direction. Repeat Steps 5 and 6 to miter each corner.

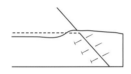

*Diagram H*

## Complete the Quilt

1. For the prairie points, refer to Diagram I. Fold each 6" red check square in half diagonally with wrong sides facing and press. Fold it in half again, forming a smaller triangle and press.

Fold line  Fold  Fold  Raw Edges

*Diagram I*

2. Pin the prairie points to the right side of the quilt top, aligning the long raw edge of each prairie point with the raw edge of the quilt top. Begin at the corner of an edge, overlapping the points slightly as shown in Diagram J by slipping the folded edge of a prairie point into the open side of the adjacent triangle. Adjust the overlap as needed to fit 14 points on each edge. Sew the points to the front.

*Diagram J*

3. Sew together the long edges of the 29-1/2x58" green check backing rectangles with a 1/2" seam allowance. Press the seam allowances to one side.

4. Smooth out the backing on a flat surface with the wrong side up and center the batting on the backing. Center the quilt top, right side up, on top of the batting. Baste the layers together.

5. Thread your machine with invisible thread and machine-quilt through all layers beginning in the center and working outward. Refer to Diagram K to quilt around each appliqué and in the ditch along all the edges of the crazy blocks and both edges of the inner border. In addition, quilt the outer border along the bottom of the red stripe and along the top of the snow banks.

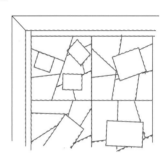

*Diagram K*

6. Trim the backing and batting even with the raw edge of the quilt top. Trim an additional 1/4" of batting from each edge. Turn the prairie points out to point away from the quilt top, folding the raw edges of the quilt top over onto the batting. Fold under 1/4" on the edges of the backing. Slip-stitch the folded edge of the backing in place or sew in the ditch around the prairie points, catching the folded edge of backing on the back of the quilt.

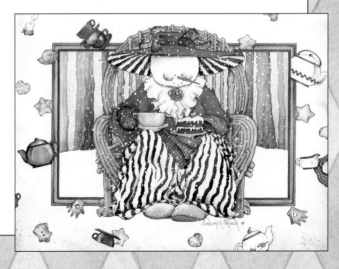

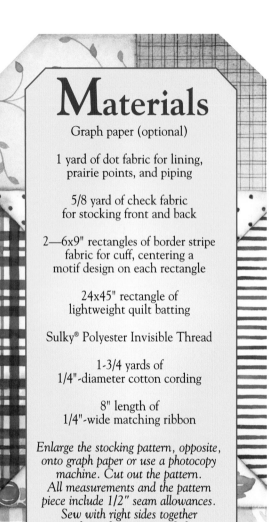

## Materials

Graph paper (optional)

1 yard of dot fabric for lining, prairie points, and piping

5/8 yard of check fabric for stocking front and back

2—6x9" rectangles of border stripe fabric for cuff, centering a motif design on each rectangle

24x45" rectangle of lightweight quilt batting

Sulky® Polyester Invisible Thread

1-3/4 yards of 1/4"-diameter cotton cording

8" length of 1/4"-wide matching ribbon

*Enlarge the stocking pattern, opposite, onto graph paper or use a photocopy machine. Cut out the pattern. All measurements and the pattern piece include 1/2" seam allowances. Sew with right sides together unless otherwise specified.*

## Quilt the Fabric

Smooth the batting on a flat surface. Center the check fabric, right side up, on the batting; pin the layers together. Thread your sewing machine with invisible thread. Machine-quilt the check fabric in a 1-1/2" diagonal grid as shown in Diagram A, using the check pattern as a guide for quilting lines.

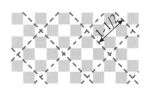

*Diagram A*

# Holiday Stocking

## Cut the Fabric

From dot, cut:

2 stocking linings, reversing one of the shapes

8—4" prairie point squares

1—6x17" cuff lining strip

1-3/4"-wide bias strips to total 60" for piping

From the quilted check, cut:

2 stockings, reversing one of the shapes

# Instructions

### Assemble the Stocking

1. To make piping, sew the short ends of the dot bias strips together to form one long piping strip. Press the seam allowances open. Center cording on the wrong side of the strip and fold fabric over the cording, matching long edges. Use a zipper foot to sew through both fabric layers close to the cording.

2. Pin the piping around the sides and foot of the stocking front so the piping stitching is on the 1/2" seam line. Baste the piping to the stocking front with a zipper foot.

3. Sew the stocking front to the back, leaving the top edges open. Trim the seam allowances and clip the curves. Turn the stocking right side out.

4. Sew the stocking lining pieces together, leaving the top edge open. Trim the seam allowances and clip the curves; do not turn.

5. Slip the lining inside stocking with wrong sides together. Baste the top edges together.

### Assemble the Cuff

1. Sew together the short edges of the cuff pieces, forming a circle. Press the seam allowances open and turn right side out.

2. For the prairie points, refer to Diagram B. Fold each 4" dot square in half diagonally with wrong sides facing and press. Fold it in half again, forming a smaller triangle and press.

 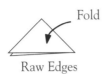

Fold line

*Diagram B*

3. Pin the prairie points to the right side of the cuff, aligning the long raw edge of each prairie point with the bottom edge of the cuff. Overlap the points slightly as shown in Diagram C by slipping the folded edge of a prairie point into the open side of the adjacent triangle. Adjust the overlap as needed to fit 8 points along the bottom edge. Sew the points to the cuff.

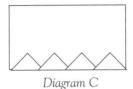

*Diagram C*

4. Sew together the short edges of the cuff lining; press the seam allowances open.

5. With right sides together, slip the cuff lining over the cuff and prairie points. Sew the cuff lining to the cuff at the bottom edge. Trim seams and turn the cuff right side out. Press and baste the top edges together.

# Complete the Stocking

1. Slip the cuff inside the stocking with the right side of the cuff facing the lining. Align the raw edges and match the seams. Sew the cuff to the stocking, easing the cuff to fit. Fold the cuff down over the right side of the stocking.

2. For the hanging loop, fold the ribbon in half. Sew the cut ends of the loop to the top inside corner on the heel side of the stocking.

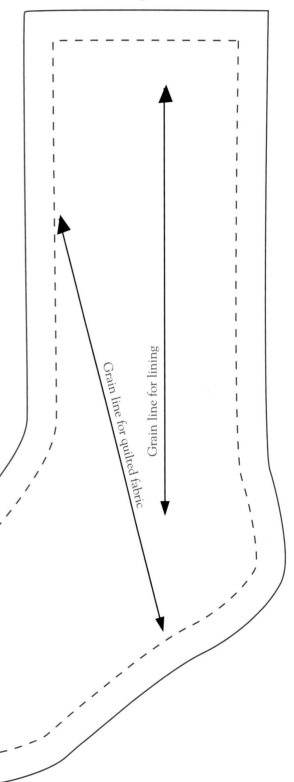

*Enlarge 300%*

Grain line for lining

Grain line for quilted fabric

# Coordinates
## *with* Patchwork

*A*  collection featuring a pre-printed fabric panel and borders often includes numerous coordinating fabrics in an array of dots, checks, stripes, plaids and prints. If you're attracted to the pre-printed fabric panel's comeplementary fabrics, the projects that follow will give you a variety of sewing options for everything from pillows to a crib bumper pad and window valance.

# Crazy-Patch Quilt

*Looking for a scrap-happy quilt? The Mother Goose character cut from a pre-printed fabric panel is surrounded by ten big blocks of irregular-shaped coordinating fabric scraps forming crazy-patch backgrounds for appliqués.*

## Materials

*Finished size: 40x51"*

1 preprinted Mother Goose quilt panel for center rectangle and appliqués

1-1/2 yards of blue stripe fabric for prairie points and blocks

1 yard of red plaid fabric for outer border

1/2 yard of blue small-print fabric for sashing and inner border

1/4 yard each of stripe fabric in green and red for blocks

1/4 yard each of plaid fabric in blue, green, and yellow for blocks

1/4 yard each of small-print fabric in cream and yellow for blocks

1/4 yard each of floral print in cream and green for blocks

1-1/2 yards of yellow medium-print fabric for backing

1-1/2 yards of muslin for foundation squares

40x52" piece of quilt batting

Sulky® Tear-Easy stabilizer

Sulky® KK 2000 temporary spray adhesive

Sulky® Rayon or Poly Deco Decorative Thread in blue, green, red, and yellow

Paper-backed fusible webbing

Sulky® Polyester Invisible Thread

*All measurements include 1/4" seam allowances. Sew with right sides together unless otherwise specified.*

## Cut the Fabric

From quilt panel, cut:
    1—10-1/2x21-1/2" Mother Goose center rectangle
    10—6" character blocks

From blue stripe, cut:
    9—4-1/4x44" strips; from the strips cut
    74—4-1/4" prairie point squares
    8 to 10 irregular-shaped pieces with straight edges

From red plaid, cut:
    1-3/4"-wide bias strips to equal a minimum of 175" for outer border

From blue small-print, cut:
    5—1-1/2x44" strips; from the strips cut
    2—32-1/2", 2—21-1/2", and 6—10-1/2" sashing strips
    4—1-1/2x44" inner border strips

From the 1/4 yard fabrics, cut:
    40 to 60 irregular-shaped pieces with straight sides

From yellow medium-print, cut:
    1—40x52" backing rectangle

From muslin, cut:
    10—12" foundation squares

From stabilizer, cut:
    10—12" squares

From fusible webbing, cut:
    10—6" squares

# Instructions

## Assemble the Crazy Blocks

1. Place a muslin foundation square on your ironing board. Select 4 to 6 irregular-shaped pieces in a variety of colors. Arrange the shapes on the foundation, completely covering the square and overlapping the edges of the shapes by a minimum of 1/2". Use Diagram A as a guide; the numbers indicate the order the shapes were placed on the foundation. Most of the blocks in our quilt use 4 larger shapes with smaller pieces layered on the larger pieces at some corners. Shapes that extend beyond the edges of the foundation square will be trimmed later.

*Diagram A*

2. Pin-baste the shapes to the foundation. Fold under 1/4" on the edges of the shapes that overlap another shape; press. In Diagram A, the bold colored lines indicated the edges that are folded under and pressed.

3. Repeat Steps 1 and 2 to make 10 crazy blocks.

4. Center a stabilizer square on the muslin side of each crazy block with temporary spray adhesive. Use a variety of decorative threads and stitches to machine-embroider along the pressed edges of the shapes, securing the shapes to the foundation squares with the stitching. Do not remove the stabilizer at this time.

5. Trim each crazy block to measure 10-1/2x10-1/2". Baste 1/4" from the raw edges.

6. Trim the 6" squares of webbing to match the shape of the preprinted character blocks. Fuse the webbing to the wrong side of the character blocks, following the manufacturer's instructions. Remove the paper backing. Center and fuse a character block on each of the crazy blocks.

7. Satin-stitch over the edges of the character blocks using your color choice of decorative thread. For an added touch, use a contrasting decorative thread to machine-buttonhole stitch directly over the satin stitching. Tear away the stabilizer from the back of the crazy blocks.

## Assemble the Quilt Center

1. Lay out the Mother Goose rectangle, crazy blocks, and sashing strips on a flat surface, using the Quilt Assembly Diagram, opposite, as a guide.

2. Sew together the crazy blocks and 10-1/2" sashing strips in the top and bottom rows as indicated in Diagram B to make 3-block units. Press the seam allowances toward the sashing.

*Diagram B*

3. Sew together the remaining blocks and 10-1/2" sashing strips as indicated in Diagram C to make 2-block units. Press the seam allowances toward the sashing.

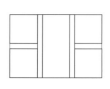

*Diagram C*

4. Use the 21-1/2" sashing strips to attach a 2-block unit from Step 3 to each long edge of the Mother Goose rectangle to complete the center section as shown in Diagram D.

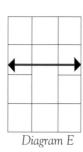

*Diagram D*

5. Use the 32-1/2" sashing strips to attach a 3-block unit from Step 2 to the top and bottom edges of the center section, using the Quilt Assembly Diagram, opposite, as a guide. Press seam allowances toward the sashing.

## Assemble the Quilt Top

1. Measure to find the quilt width through the center as shown in Diagram E. Cut two 1-1/2"-wide blue print inner border strips to this length. Sew the inner borders to the top and bottom edges of the quilt center. Press the seam allowances toward the borders.

*Diagram E*

2. Measure the quilt length through the center including the borders as shown in Diagram F. Seam the 1-1/2"-wide blue print inner border strips as needed to make two this length. Sew the inner borders to the left and right edges of the quilt. Press the seam allowances toward the borders.

*Diagram F*

3. Using the length found in Step 2, seam the 1-3/4"-wide red plaid outer border strips as needed to make two this length. Referring to the Quilt Assembly Diagram, below right, sew the outer borders to the left and right edges of the quilt. Press the seam allowances toward the outer borders.

4. Measure the quilt width, including all borders. Cut two outer borders to this length from the remaining 1-3/4"-wide red plaid strips. Sew the outer borders to the top and bottom edges of the quilt. Press the seam allowances toward the outer borders.

## Complete the Quilt

1. For the prairie points, refer to Diagram G. Fold each 4-1/4" blue stripe square in half diagonally with wrong sides facing and press. Fold it in half again, forming a smaller triangle and press.

*Diagram G*

2. Pin the prairie points to the right side of the quilt top, aligning the long raw edge of each prairie point with the raw edge of the quilt top. Begin at the corner of an edge, overlapping the points slightly as shown in Diagram H by slipping the folded edge of a prairie point into the open side of the adjacent tri-angle. Adjust the overlap as needed to fit 21 points on each side edge and 16 on the top and bottom edges. Sew the points to the front.

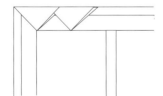

*Diagram H*

3. Smooth out the backing on a flat surface with the wrong side up and center the batting on the backing. Center the quilt top, right side up, on top of the batting. Baste the layers together.

4. Thread your machine with invisible thread and machine-quilt through all layers beginning in the center and working outward. Refer to Diagram I to

quilt around each appliqué and in the ditch along the edges of the sashing and inner border. In addition, our quilt was machine-quilted to outline Mother Goose in the center rectangle.

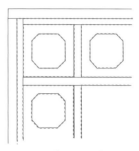

*Diagram I*

5. Trim the backing and batting even with the raw edge of the quilt top. Trim an additional 1/4" of batting from each edge. Turn the prairie points out to point away from the quilt top, folding the raw edges of the quilt top over onto the batting. Fold under 1/4" on the edges of the backing. Slip-stitch the folded edge of the backing in place or sew in the ditch along the prairie points, catching the folded edge of backing on the back of the quilt.

*Quilt Assembly Diagram*

# Pick a Pillow

*If this little piggy went to market to pick a pack of pillows he is in for a treat, and so are you! On the following pages help yourself to a big batch of pillows— from box to bolster—all featuring character motifs and coordinating fabrics.*

## Materials

3/4 yard of floral print fabric
for back and sides

1/2 yard of red plaid fabric for center
square and piping

Border stripe fabric
for front border strips

1—6" character block from preprinted
Mother Goose panel for appliqué

6" square of fusible webbing

12" square of Sulky® Tear-Easy stabilizer

Sulky® KK 2000
temporary spray adhesive

Sulky® Rayon or Poly Deco Decorative
Thread in green and red

4 1/4 yards of narrow cotton cording

3x18x18" box pillow form

*All measurements include 1/2" seam
allowances. Sew with right sides
together unless otherwise specified.*

## Box Pillow

### Cut the Fabric

From floral print, cut:
- 1—19" back square
- 2—4x38" side strips

From red plaid, cut:
- 1—10-1/2" center front square
- 1-1/2"-wide bias strips to total 150" of piping

From border stripe, cut:
- 4—5-1/4x24" front border strips, planning the design placement

### Instructions

1. To miter the border, pin a 5-1/4x24" front border strip to the red plaid center front square, matching the center of the strip and the center of the square. Sew together, beginning and ending the seam 1/2" from the edges of the center square as shown in Diagram A.

Repeat with each border strip. Trim the seam allowances to 1/4" and press toward the border strips.

*Diagram A*

2. Working with one corner at a time, draw a diagonal line on the wrong side of the top strip from the corner of the stitching to the point where the two strips meet at the raw edges as shown in Diagram B. Reposition the strips so the bottom strip is on top and draw a second line in the same manner.

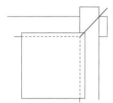

*Diagram B*

3. With right sides together, match the drawn lines and pin as shown in Diagram C. Beginning at the inside corner, sew the strips together directly on the drawn lines. Trim the excess fabric, leaving a 1/4" seam allowance. Press the seam allowances open. Repeat Steps 2 and 3 to miter each corner.

*Diagram C*

4. Trim the 6" square of webbing to match the shape of the preprinted character block. Fuse the webbing to the wrong side of the block, following the manufacturer's instructions. Remove the paper backing. Center and fuse the block on the pillow front.

5. Center the 12" square of tear-away stabilizer behind the red plaid center square on the back of the pillow front with temporary spray adhesive. Satin-stitch over the edges of the block and the center square with green decorative thread. For an added touch, use red decorative thread to machine-buttonhole stitch directly over the green satin stitching. Tear away the stabilizer from the back of the pillow front.

6. To make piping, sew the short ends of the piping strips together to form one long strip. Press the seam allowances open. Center cording on wrong side of strip and fold fabric over the cording, matching long edges. Use a zipper foot to sew through both fabric layers close to the cording.

7. Beginning at the center bottom of the pillow front, pin piping to the right side of the front, slightly rounding corners with raw edges facing out. Clip seam allowance of piping at corners for a better fit. Overlap ends of piping, trimming off excess piping. Baste piping to pillow front using zipper foot. Repeat for pillow back.

8. Sew the short ends of the side bands together to form one long side strip. Press the seam allowances open and press under 1-1/2" at one end. Pin the side band to the right side of the pillow front, beginning with the pressed end at the center of the bottom edge; trim the opposite end to overlap the pressed end.

9. Sew the side band to pillow front as shown in Diagram D, sewing atop the piping basting stitches, and clipping seam allowance of side band as you sew for a better fit. Sew together the overlapped area on the opposite edge of the side band to secure the band's correct length.

*Diagram D*

10. Sew the opposite edge of the side band to the pillow back in the same manner, taking care to position the pillow back corners in line with the pillow front corners and leaving a 10" opening in the bottom edge.

11. Turn the pillow cover right side out. Insert the pillow form and sew the opening closed.

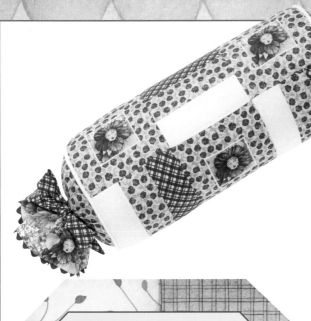

# Bolster Pillow

## Cut the Fabric

From border stripe, cut:

    2—4x24-1/2" border strips

    6—3" motif squares, centering the motif in the square

From floral print, cut:

    6—6-1/2" squares

    6—2-1/2x6-1/2" block strips

    2—4-1/2x24-1/2" end strips

    2—4x24-1/2" lining strips

From red plaid, cut:

    6—2-1/2x6-1/2" bias-cut block strips

    2—3-1/2x34" bias-cut tie strips

From white-on-white, cut:

    6—2-1/2x6-1/2" block strips

    2—1-1/2x28" piping strips

From fusible webbing, cut:

    6—3" squares

From Tear-Easy stabilizer, cut:

    6—5" squares

*Sew with right sides together using 1/4" seam allowances unless otherwise specified.*

## Instructions

### Assemble the Pillow Center

1.  Fuse a webbing square to the wrong side of each motif square, following the manufacturer's instructions. Remove the paper backing. Center and fuse a motif square on each 6-1/2" floral print square.

2.  Center a 5" square of stabilizer behind the motif square on the back of each 6-1/2" floral print square with temporary spray adhesive. Satin-stitch over the edges of the motif square with white decorative thread. Tear away the stabilizer from the back of the floral print square.

### Materials

1-1/2 yards of border stripe fabric, with two of the selected borders per width of fabric

3/4 yard of floral print fabric

3/4 yard of red plaid fabric

1/4 yard of white-on-white fabric

20x26" piece of quilt batting

1-1/2 yards of narrow cotton cording

Paper-backed fusible webbing

Sulky® Tear-Easy stabilizer

Sulky® KK 2000 temporary spray adhesive

Sulky® Rayon or Poly Deco Decorative Thread in white

1-1/2 yards of red rick-rack

Polyester fiberfill

2 rubber bands

3. Join the 2-1/2x6-1/2" block strips in sets of three as shown in Diagram A, using one strip of each fabric with the floral print in the center. Press the seam allowances to the same side.

*Diagram A*

4. Lay out the pieced blocks and the appliquéd floral squares in four rows of three blocks, alternating the direction of the pieced blocks from row to row as shown in Diagram B.

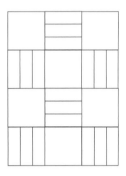

*Diagram B*

5. When you are pleased with the arrangement, sew the blocks together in rows. Press the seam allowances of each row to one side, alternating the direction with each row.

6. Sew the rows together to complete the pillow cover center.

## Complete the Pillow Center

1. Smooth out the 20x26" piece of batting on a flat surface and center the pillow cover center right side up on the batting. Baste the layers together 1/4" from the edges of the pillow cover center.

2. Thread your machine with invisible thread and machine-quilt through all layers, sewing in the ditch of each seam as shown in Diagram C.

*Diagram C*

3. To make piping, center cording on the wrong side of each 1-1/2x28" piping strip and fold fabric over the cording, matching long edges. Use a zipper foot to sew through both fabric layers close to the cording.

4. Pin a piping strip along each 24-1/2" edge on the right side of the pillow center so the piping stitching is on the 1/4" seam line. Baste the piping to the pillow center using a zipper foot.

5. Sew the remaining edges of the pillow center together, forming a tube. Press the seam allowance open and turn the pillow center right side out.

## Complete the Pillow Cover

1. Align the top edge of a 4x24-1/2" border strip with a long edge of a 4-1/2x24-1/2" floral end strip; sew the long edges together. Press the seam allowances toward the border strip. Repeat for the remaining border and floral end strip.

2. Position rick-rack along the remaining long edge on the right side of each border strip as shown in Diagram D. Baste in place with the center of the rick-rack on the 1/4" seam line.

*Diagram D*

3. Sew together the short edges of each border/end strip, forming a circle. Press the seam allowances open.

4. Sew together the short edges of each lining strip, forming a circle. Press the seam allowances open and press under a scant 1/4" on one raw edge of each lining.

5. With right sides facing, slip a lining over each of the border/end pieces, aligning the raw edge of the lining with the rick-rack edge of the border; sew. Fold the lining down over the wrong side of the border/end piece to cover the machine stitching; press. Slip-stitch the pressed edge in place or sew in the ditch along the border, catching the pressed edge of the lining in the stitching.

6. With right sides facing, slip a border/end piece over the pillow center, aligning the raw edge of the end piece with the piped edge of the pillow center; sew together with a zipper foot. Pull the border/end piece away from the pillow center; press. Repeat for other end.

7. To make a tie, fold a 3-1/2x34" red plaid strip in half lengthwise with right sides together. Diagonally trim the strip ends as shown in Diagram E. Sew the raw edges together, leaving a 2" opening for turning. Trim the seam, turn right side out, and press. Sew the opening closed. Repeat for the second tie.

*Diagram E*

8. Stuff the pillow cover with polyester fiberfill. Secure each end with a rubber band. Use the ties to make a bow over each rubber band.

# Materials

1-3/4 yard of green print fabric for pieced border and back

1-1/4 yards of green stripe fabric for squares, blocks, and binding

1/2 yard of blue plaid fabric for block and pieced border

1 fat quarter or 1/4 yard each of red and yellow plaid fabric for blocks

Quilt batting

Sulky® Polyester Invisible Thread

18" length of 3/4"-wide sew on hook-and-loop fastener

26x26" pillow form

*All measurements include 1/4" seam allowances. Sew with right sides together unless otherwise specified.*

# Purely Patchwork Pillow

## Cut the Fabric

From green print, cut:

    4—1-1/2x44" strips; from the strips cut

    2—28" and 2—26" inner border strips

    4—2-1/2x44" strips; from the strips cut

    56—2-1/2" border squares

    2—18x32" back rectangles

From green stripe, cut:

    4—9" squares

    10—5-1/8" block squares

    2-3/4"-wide bias strips to total 144" of binding

From blue plaid, cut:

    2—5-1/8" block squares

    4—2-1/2x44"strips; from the strips cut

    32—2-1/2x4-1/2" border rectangles

From red plaid, cut:

    4—5-1/8" block squares

From yellow plaid, cut:

    4—5-1/8" block squares

From batting, cut:

    1—34" square

    2—17-1/2x32" rectangles

# Instructions

## Assemble the Pinwheel Blocks

1. With right sides together, layer the 5-1/8" squares in pairs, using a green stripe with each of the plaid squares. Cut the layered squares in half diagonally as shown in Diagram A to make 20 sets of triangles.

Diagram A

2. Sew 1/4" from the diagonal edge of each pair to make a square as shown in Diagram B. Press the seam allowances toward the striped triangles.

Diagram B

3. Arrange sets of four squares as shown in Diagram C. Sew the squares together in rows and then sew the rows together to make 5 pinwheel blocks.

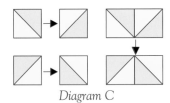

Diagram C

## Assemble the Pillow Front Center

1. Lay out the pinwheel blocks and the 9" green stripe squares in three rows of three blocks, using Diagram D as a guide.

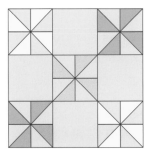

Diagram D

2. Sew the blocks together in rows. Press the seam allowances of each row to one side, alternating the direction with each row.

3. Sew the rows together to complete the pillow front center. Press the seam allowances toward the center row.

## Complete the Pillow Front

1. Sew a 1-1/2x26" green print inner border strip to opposite edges of the pillow front center. Press the seam allowances toward the border.

2. Sew a 1-1/2x28" green print inner border to each of the remaining edges of the pillow front center. Press the seam allowances toward the border.

3. With right sides facing, place a 2-1/2" green print square on the corner of a 2-1/2x4-1/2" blue plaid rectangle. Draw a diagonal line on the square as shown in Diagram E. Sew on the drawn line and trim the seam allowance to 1/4". Press the seam allowance toward the green print triangle.

Diagram E

4. Sew another green print square to the opposite corner of the blue plaid rectangle in the same manner, creating a 3-piece unit as shown in Diagram F. Repeat to make a total of 24—3-piece units.

Diagram F

5. Refer to Diagram G to make the two-piece corner units. Use the same method as in Step 3 to sew green print squares onto the left end only of 4 blue plaid rectangles. Then sew green print squares onto the right end only of the remaining 4 blue plaid rectangles.

Diagram G

6. Lay out six 3-piece units and two corner units as shown in Diagram H. Sew the units together to make a pieced border. Check the length of the pieced border against an inner border and adjust the seam allowances if needed to fit. Repeat to make a total of four pieced borders.

Diagram H

7. Sew a pieced border to an inner border, beginning and ending the seam 1/4" from the edges of the inner border as shown in Diagram I. Repeat with each pieced border. Press the seam allowances toward the inner border.

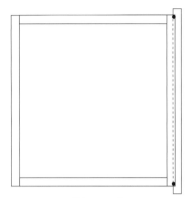

*Diagram I*

8. Working with one corner at a time, draw a diagonal line on the wrong side of the 2-piece corner unit from the stitching to the point where the two pieced borders meet at the raw edges as shown in Diagram J. Reposition the borders so the bottom border is on top and draw a second line in the same manner.

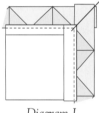

*Diagram J*

9. With right sides together, match the drawn lines and pin as shown in Diagram K. Beginning at the inside corner, sew the borders together directly on the drawn lines. Trim the excess fabric, leaving a 1/4" seam allowance. Press the seam allowances one direction. Repeat Steps 8 and 9 to miter each corner.

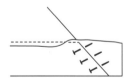

*Diagram K*

# Complete the Pillow Cover

1. Smooth out the batting square on a flat surface and center the pillow front, right side up, on top of the batting. Baste the layers together.

2. Thread your machine with invisible thread and machine-quilt in the ditch along all edges of the pinwheel blocks and the pieced border as shown in

Diagram L. Trim the batting even with the raw edge of the pillow front.

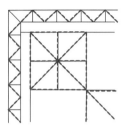

*Diagram L*

3. Smooth an 18x32" green print back rectangle onto each of the batting rectangles, aligning three of the edges; baste along the three aligned edges. Fold the fabric over the batting on the remaining edge and sew 1/4" from the fold.

4. Smooth the pillow front, right side down, on a flat surface. Position a back rectangle right side up on the pillow front, aligning three edges with the folded edge near the center. Position the remaining back rectangle over the remaining half of the pillow front in the same manner. Pin, then sew the overlapped areas of the back together at the edges; do not sew to the front at this time.

5. Sew the hook side of the fastener on the wrong side of the upper back piece, centering it along the folded edge. Mark the location for the loop side of the fastener on the right side of the lower back piece and sew the fastener in place.

6. Reposition the back on the front with wrong sides facing and pin together. Use invisible thread to sew through all layers, quilting in the ditch along both edges of the inner border as shown in Diagram M.

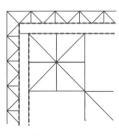

*Diagram M*

7. Sew the short ends of the 2-3/4"-wide green stripe binding strips together with diagonal seams to form

one long binding strip. Trim the seam allowances to 1/4" and press open. Fold the strip in half lengthwise with wrong sides together; press.

8. Beginning at the center of one edge of the pillow cover, place the binding strip on the right side of the pillow front, aligning the raw edges of the binding with the raw edges of the pillow cover. Fold over the beginning of the binding strip about 1/2". Sew through all layers 1/4" from the raw edges, mitering the corners. Trim away the excess binding, leaving 1/2" at the end to overlap the beginning of the strip.

9. Fold the binding to the back of the pillow to cover the machine stitching; press. Slip-stitch the folded edge of the binding in place or sew in the ditch along the binding, catching the folded edge of the binding on the back of the pillow.

10. Insert the pillow form in the cover through the hook and loop fastener opening.

---

# Materials

1/2 yard of yellow print fabric

1/4 yard of red plaid fabric

1/8 yard of red stripe fabric

Fabric with motif to fill a 4" square for front center

14x14" pillow form

# Multi-Patch Pillow
## Cut the Fabric

From yellow print, cut:
    1—16" back square
    12—4" front squares

From red plaid, cut:
    8—4" bias-cut front squares

From red stripe, cut:
    4—4" front squares

From motif fabric, cut:
    1—4" center front square,
    centering the motif in the square

*Sew with WRONG sides together using 1/2" seam allowances unless otherwise specified.*

## Instructions

1. Lay out the 4" squares on a flat surface in 5 rows of 5 squares. Place the motif square in the center and alternate stripe and print squares around the center square, followed by alternating plaid and print squares.

2. Sew the squares together in rows, and then sew the rows together to complete the pillow front.

3. To fringe, make 1/4" to 3/8" cuts 1/4" apart along the sewn seams of the pillow front.

4. Sew the pillow front to the back, leaving an 8" opening in the bottom edge.

5. Insert the pillow form into the pillow cover. Use a zipper foot to sew the opening closed, sewing 1/2" from the raw edges. Fringe the outer seam allowances of the pillow cover as in Step 3.

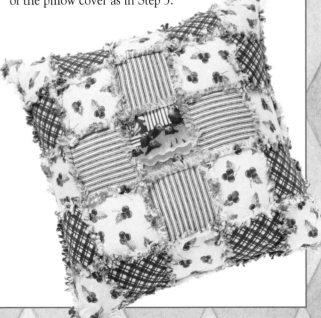

# Crib Bumper Pad

*A securely-tied bumper pad can protect a newborn from drafts,
or you can use the shortened version shown on page 93 as decor
above the crib or to brighten a nearby wall.*

## Materials

*Finished size: 9-3/4x180"*

Preprinted alphabet block quilt panel
for appliqué

2 yards of green stripe fabric

1-1/2 yards of red check fabric

1/3 yard of green small floral fabric

1/3 yard of pink small floral fabric

1/3 yard of green check fabric

1/3 yard of pink check fabric

1/3 yard of blue check fabric

1/3 yard of blue stripe fabric

1/3 yard of yellow small floral fabric

1/3 yard of yellow stripe fabric

2/3 yard of 90"-wide high loft batting

11 yards of narrow cotton cording

Sulky® Tear-Easy™ stabilizer

Sulky® KK 2000 temporary spray adhesive

Sulky® Puffy Foam™
in blue, green, red, and yellow

Sulky® Rayon or Poly Deco™
thread in coordinating
blue, green, red, and yellow

Paper-backed fusible webbing

Air-erasable fabric markers

Sulky® Polyester Invisible Thread

*All measurements include 1/4" seam
allowances. Sew with right sides
together unless otherwise specified.*

## Cut the Fabric

From quilt panel, cut:
>   4—6-1/4" alphabet block squares

From green stripe, cut:
>   6—10-3/4x30-1/4" back rectangles
>   2—10-3/4" front squares

From red check, cut:
>   1-1/2"-wide bias strips to equal 19 yards for
>   piping and ties

From green small floral, cut:
>   2—12" letter squares

From pink small floral, cut:
>   2—12" letter squares

From each of the remaining 1/3 yard fabrics, cut:
>   2—10-3/4" front squares

From batting, cut:
>   2—10-3/4x90" strips

From fusible webbing, cut:
>   4—6-1/4" squares

## Instructions

### Assemble the Front

1.  Cut eight 12" squares of tear-away stabilizer. Use temporary spray
    adhesive to center two layers of stabilizer on the back of each 12"
    green and pink letter square. Machine-embroider a 5"-tall letter
    centered on each of the stabilized squares using decorative thread and
    matching Puffy Foam. Embroider a red letter and a yellow letter on the

green squares. Embroider a blue letter and a green letter on the pink squares. Tear away the stabilizer. Trim each embroidered square into a 10-3/4" square, centering the letter. For more information about embroidering, refer to pages 60 and 61.

2. Sew together the 10-3/4" yellow floral and blue stripe squares and the blue check and green stripe squares in pairs as shown in Diagram A. Press all seam allowances open.

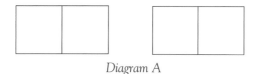

*Diagram A*

3. Fuse a square of webbing to the wrong side of each 6-1/4" alphabet block square, following the manufacturer's instructions. Remove the paper backing. Center an alphabet block on each pair of 10-3/4" squares from Step 2 as shown in Diagram B. Fuse the blocks in place.

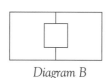

*Diagram B*

4. Use temporary spray adhesive to center an 8" square of tear-away stabilizer behind the fused block on the back of each square pair. Satin-stitch over the edges of each alphabet block with red decorative thread. Tear away the stabilizer.

5. Refer to Diagram C and the instructions that follow to sew together the 10-3/4" squares. Begin with a green check, followed by a yellow floral/blue stripe pair, pink check, green embroidered, yellow stripe, blue check/green stripe pair, pink embroidered, green check, yellow floral/blue stripe pair, pink check, green embroidered, yellow stripe, blue check/green stripe pair, and end with a pink embroidered square.

*Diagram C*

6. Sew the short ends of the red check piping strips together to form two 178" piping strips. Press the seam allowances open. Center cording on the wrong side of each strip and fold fabric over the cording, matching long edges. Use a zipper foot to sew through both fabric layers close to the cording.

7. Pin a piping strip along each long edge on the right side of the pieced front so the piping stitching is on the 1/2" seam line. Baste piping to the front using a zipper foot.

8. From the remaining red check bias strips, cut thirty-two 10" lengths for ties. Fold each tie strip in half lengthwise with right sides together. Sew with a 1/4" seam allowance, leaving one short edge open for turning. Trim the seam allowance to 1/8", turn right side out, and press.

9. Pin the ties to the right side of the pieced front where indicated by dots in Diagram D, aligning the raw edges. Place a single tie at each corner of the pieced front and pairs of ties at all remaining dots. Repeat for the remaining three sides. Sew the ties in place.

*Diagram D*

## Complete the Bumper Pad

1. Sew together the short edges of the 10-3/4x30-1/4" back rectangles to make one long back. Press the seam allowances open.

2. Place batting on the wrong side of the back, overlapping the short edges of the batting at the center of the back. Baste a scant 1/2" from the edges and trim the batting close to the stitching.

3. Pin pieced front to back with right sides together. Sew front to back, leaving one short edge open. Turn right side out and slip-stitch the opening closed.

4. Thread your sewing machine with Sulky® Polyester Invisible Thread in both the needle and the bobbin. Machine-quilt through all layers at each vertical seam of the front squares; do not quilt at the center of the appliquéd pairs.

## Materials

1-1/4 yard of bumper stripe fabric for front

1/2 yard of blue stripe fabric for border and backing

1/2 yard of yellow plaid fabric for piping and ties

2-1/2 yards of 3/8" cotton cording

13x44" piece of high loft batting

Sulky® Polyester Invisible Thread

*All measurements include 1/2" seam allowances. Sew with right sides together unless otherwise specified.*

## Cut the Fabric

From bumper stripe, cut:
   1—11x44" strip

From blue stripe, cut:
   1—3x44" border strip
   1—13x44" backing

From yellow plaid, cut:
   2"-wide bias strips to equal 7 yards for piping and ties

## Instructions

1. Sew the blue stripe border strip to the top edge of the bumper stripe strip. Press the seam allowances toward the border.

# Crib Topper

2. Sew the short ends of the yellow plaid bias strips together to form two 45" piping strips. Press the seam allowances open. Center cording on the wrong side of each strip and fold fabric over the cording, matching long edges. Use a zipper foot to sew through both fabric layers close to the cording.

3. Pin a piping strip along each long edge on the right side of the topper front so the piping stitching is on the 1/2" seam line. Baste piping to the front using a zipper foot.

4. From the remaining yellow plaid bias strips, cut twelve 12" lengths for ties. Fold each tie strip in half lengthwise with right sides together. Sew with a 1/2" seam allowance, leaving one short edge open for turning. Trim the seam allowance to 1/4", turn right side out, and press.

5. Pin the ties in pairs to the right side of the topper front at each corner and at the center of each long edge, aligning the raw edges. Sew the ties in place.

6. Place batting on the wrong side of the backing. Baste a scant 1/2" from the edges and trim the batting close to the stitching.

7. Sew the topper front to the back, leaving one short edge open. Turn right side out and sew the opening closed.

8. Thread your sewing machine with invisible thread. Machine-quilt in the ditch along the bottom edge of the blue stripe border.

# Window Valance

*For a custom window treatment, combine a coordinating fabric with an all-over toss design and ticking stripe fabric to make the valance. Dress up purchased sheers with easily-appliquéd animal blocks cut from a pre-printed fabric panel.*

◆◆●◆◆

## Materials

Blue stripe fabric

Yellow print fabric

White lining fabric

Air-erasable fabric marker

Ruler

## Cut the Fabric

1. Measure the length of your curtain rod, including the side returns if they will be covered by the valance. Multiple this number by 1-1/2 or 2 to determine the finished valance width.

2. Divide the finished valance width number from Step 1 by the width of the fabric, then round up to the nearest whole number for the number of fabric widths needed.

3. Multiply the number of fabric widths from Step 2 by 17-1/2" (the width of the strips) to determine the amount of blue stripe fabric to purchase and by 15-1/2" (the width of the strips) to determine the amount of yellow print and white lining fabric to purchase.

4. Using the number determined in Step 2, cut 17-1/2"-wide strips from the blue stripe fabric and 15-1/2"-wide strips from the yellow print and lining fabrics.

## Instructions

1. Sew the 15-1/2" edges of the yellow print strips together to form one long strip. Press the seam allowances open. Repeat for the lining strips.

2. Place the yellow strip, right side up, on a flat surface. Position the lining strip, right side down, on the yellow strip. Referring to Diagram A, use an air-erasable fabric marker to make a mark on the lining 5" from the left edge and 7-1/2" from the top edge. Repeat at the opposite end of lining.

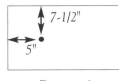

7-1/2"

5"

*Diagram A*

3. Continue making a row of evenly spaced marks 7-1/2" from the top edge and approximately 11" apart as shown in Diagram B. The number and spacing will vary depending on the width of your valance.

*Diagram B*

4. Make a mark 5/8" from the bottom edge and 1/2" in from each short edge of the lining. Continue making a row of marks 5/8" from the bottom edge, positioning each mark so it is centered between the marks in the upper row as shown in Diagram C.

*Diagram C*

5. Using a ruler and fabric marker, connect the dots in a zigzag-fashion as shown in Diagram D. Pin the lining to the yellow print overlay on the drawn lines and along the short edges. Sew the strips together on the drawn lines and 1/2" from the short edges. Trim the seam allowances to 1/4". Turn the overlay right side out and press. Baste the top edges together.

*Diagram D*

6. Sew the 17-1/2" edges of the blue stripe strips together to make one long valance strip. Press the seam allowances open.

7. Measuring from end to end, find the finished width of the yellow print overlay; add 2". Use this number to trim the blue stripe strip. For side hems, fold over 1/2" twice on each short edge of the blue stripe valance; press. Edge-stitch close to the inner pressed edge shown in Diagram E.

*Diagram E*

8. For bottom hem, press under 1/2" and then 1" on the bottom edge of the blue stripe valance. Edge-stitch close to the inner pressed edge.

9. With the right side of the yellow print overlay facing the wrong side of the blue stripe valance, align the top edges. Sew the top edges together using a 1/2" seam allowance.

10. Fold the yellow overlay down over the right side of the blue stripe valance; press. Refer to Diagram F to make the rod pocket, sewing 2" from the top and then 2" from the first line of stitching.

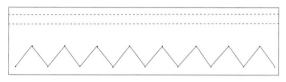

*Diagram F*